LEADERSHIP COMPASS

12 Steps to Becoming a Purposeful Leader

S M A MOIN

Leadership Compass: 12 Steps to Becoming a Purposeful Leader

Copyright © 2020 S M A Moin

All rights reserved.

The moral rights of the author have been asserted. As part of the full rights of copyright, no part of this publication can be reproduced, transmitted in any form by any means, including electronic, mechanical, information storage, retrieval systems, photocopying, recording or other means of storage without the prior written permission of the copyright owner and the author mentioned above.

ISBN: 9781673879063

Published by Amazon.com. Inc. through KDP

To those leaders who put God first, their people second, and themselves last.

Other Books by Dr S M A Moin

The Purpose of Life: Understanding the Divine Message through the Lens of Leadership and Strategy

Creativity in the Imagination Age: Theories, Practice and Application

Digital Robin Hood: The Persecution of an Innocent Soul

Brand Storytelling in the Digital Age: Theories, Practice and Application

Strategy Made Easy: Introducing a New Strategy Model, Saarbrücken, Germany: Lambert Academic Publishing.

CONTENTS

Foreword vi

INTRODUCTION

The Journey: Let Faith Chart Your Course — 3
The Leadership Compass: 12 Transformational Steps — 19

I. CLARITY

1. Know Your Lord: Put God First — 51
2. Know Yourself: Meet God's Lieutenant — 67
3. Know Your Purpose: Set Your Moral Gyro — 85

II. COMMITMENT

4. Assume Command: Take the Helm of Your Life — 101
5. Seek Guidance: Find Freedom through Faith — 117
6. Be a Lifelong Learner: Develop the Third Eye — 131

III. TRANSFORMATION

7. Live Like a Traveller: Find Abundance in Less — 159
8. Have an Attitude of Gratitude: Focus Your Eyes on the Prize — 173
9. Persevere with Patience and Prayer: Transform through Struggles — 181

IV. IMPACT

10. Start with a Dream: Navigate with a Vision — 199
11. Embark on a Mission: Make Service Part of Every Day — 211
12. Lead with Character: Bring Values to Life — 223
Epilogue — 241
References — 245
Index — 253
Acknowledgment — 258
About The Author — 259

FOREWORD

Leadership influences all aspects of our lives. It is one of the widely studied, mostly misunderstood subjects that determines the success or failure of the teams, organisations, societies, and countries at large. Leadership Compass: 12 Steps to Becoming a Purposeful Leader challenges conventional leadership thinking drawing on leadership experience from the sea and the shore while reflecting on the lessons learned from different industries. The book critically approaches leadership from multidisciplinary perspectives and draws from the teachings of the Divine Scripture, linking leadership with the purpose of life.

This book introduces a leadership compass that will set forth anyone on a journey to become a purpose-driven leader following twelve transformational steps and can be used by strategic leaders in the boardroom and by the aspiring leaders at the bootcamp. Concentrating on worldly life, many leaders use their title and authority while influencing their followers and define their success by their position and power. Leadership Compass, on the other hand, sees 'life' beyond death, bringing eternal life into the picture.

While the Great Man theory of leadership posits that people born with leadership traits become leaders, other theories suggest that leadership can be learned. In contrast, the author takes a stance that every human being is born as Lieutenant (Khalifa) of God, who is the Creator (al-Khaliq) of this universe. From that perspective, every human being is a leader with the responsibility to manifest the grand purpose of life. Drawing on the teachings of the Divine Scripture, the author explains the purpose of life in two simple terms: submission to God and service to humanity, inviting the readers to be purposeful leaders. Leadership is a quest, and great leaders never stop learning. Leadership Compass promotes the value of learning, encouraging leaders to learn with an open mind, and become humble to unlearn and relearn. The book has fifteen chapters, including the prologue. The first quadrant of the compass is 'Clarity', (Part I) which involves a quest to gain a deeper understanding of the purpose for which human beings are created. In search of the meaning of life, the author has changed the big question from "why am I here?" to "why am I created?" This leads him to explore the domains of theology and philosophy. Can you think of a fulfilling life without knowing its purpose? If leaders do not know their purpose, how can they lead others in the right direction?

The second quadrant of the leadership compass is 'Commitment' (Part II), implying a commitment to grow through three key steps: taking the helm of your life, seeking guidance, and becoming a lifelong learner. The book focused on two kinds of knowledge: Divine and secular knowledge. Divine knowledge helps humankind to reflect on the cosmological signatures in the universe and understand the dynamics of Lord-lieutenant and Master-slave relationships. Secular knowledge includes the domains of science, management, economics, geography, politics, and so on. Seeking both kinds of knowledge is critical for developing wisdom and insights through which leaders create their third eye: the Gut.

The third quadrant of the leadership compass is 'Transformation' (Part III), at the hearts of which are hardships and struggles. Human beings grow through suffering, and our character reveals when we are tested. We are not made by our circumstances but by how we respond to adversities. All great leaders have developed their character through struggles that have given them the courage and confidence to stand for the right cause. The transformational journey will unveil how to find abundance in less, remain grateful, go through struggles, and turn adversities into opportunities. The fourth quadrant of the leadership compass is 'Impact' (Part IV), which differentiates the leaders from the crowd. Leaders need to make an impact in the lives of the people they are entrusted to serve. Leadership is not about creating followers, but developing leaders who inspire, motivate, and mobilize people on a mission. Particular emphasis is given on leaders' character, which is defined by the values and principles leaders live with. It is the character, not charisma that helps the leaders win the trust of their people. Leaders with character inspire and motivate, but leaders without character manipulate. The author argues that the real leaders with genuine character make them accountable to their Creator and focus on the rights of their people instead of their position and authority. Leadership Compass will guide you to assume the command of your life and embark you on a transformational journey to becoming a purposeful leader.

Finally, the book will help you to create your legacy as a leader but remember, as William Shakespeare said, "No legacy is so rich as honesty". No matter which step of leadership ladder you are at the moment, Leadership Compass will help you assume the command of your life and embark you on a transformational journey.

Admiral Aurangzeb Chowdhury
Former Chief of Naval Staff
Bangladesh Navy

INTRODUCTION

"On a journey the leader of people is their servant"

PROPHET MUHAMMAD (PBUH)

THE JOURNEY
Let Faith Chart Your Course

When I was a Year VII student, I read a Bengali poem titled *'Twelve Seas'* taken from the book: *'The Sailor of the Seven Seas,'* written by a famous Bengali poet *Farrukh Ahmad*. The poem portrays the vivid experience of a voyage of a valiant sailor into the rough sea during a stormy night. He lost one of his hands while controlling the helm of the boat, but this undoubtedly painful incident could not deviate him from his mission as he did not lose hope and had complete trust in God. Therefore, he took over the helm with his other hand, setting the course of the boat towards the harbour. He encountered cyclonic winds and high waves that placed him in further danger, on edge between life and death.

This was the first time that I had come across the concept of leadership. Reciting this poem time and again, I could decode some of the valuable leadership traits. The teachings of the poem persuaded me to believe that leaders are the ones who have absolute clarity about their mission, a deep sense of responsibility for their people, and the properties under their disposal. But most importantly, good leaders put their complete trust upon their Lord, so they never lose the courage to throw themselves into significant challenges.

The poem was a source of inspiration until I joined the Navy and also throughout my naval career. Embarking upon the life of a sailor opened many doors for me for a never-ending journey to leadership. I was fascinated by the topic. Eventually, I read many books and articles on leadership, management, and strategy. At some point, reading about leadership became my hobby, and my quest to learn and understand the nature of leadership has never stopped. I tried to comprehend leadership in different ways: by *reading, reflecting, observing, and practicing.* Besides reading, I have deeply reflected on my own life: *the struggles I have gone through and the lessons I have learned from life experience.* When I was undertaking my midshipman training on-board warships, I was introduced to a common saying: *"When the going gets tough, the tough gets going."* I have also read the life experience of many senior business executives, political icons, Olympic athletes, football coaches, and spiritual leaders. In search of leadership gems, at some point, I consulted the Divine message, the Qur'an, and the life of the Messengers of God. I felt a sense of guilt in my heart when I came across Michael H. Hart's book, *"The 100: A Ranking of the Most Influential Persons in History"*. I had spent so many years of my life trying to understand leadership in numerous ways, but I had never taken an in-depth look into the life of the person who topped the list. He has not just brought the last revelation of God, he was also sent by God as the mercy to all the creations: *"And We have not sent you, [O Muhammad], except as a mercy to the worlds."* (Qur'an 21: 107).

This verse along with many other verses of the Qur'an taught me the role and status of the last Messenger of God, Muhammad (PBUH). Lately, I have realised what I was missing by not learning from the life of Muhammad (PBUH) and the message he brought for the whole of humankind. You may have noticed that the word 'world' is plural (i.e. worlds) in this verse. Initially I was confused but when I read the explanation of this verse, I understood that this was not a mistake. Indeed, in this context, the word 'worlds' refers to all the nations in different parts of the world that came before, are living currently, and will be coming in the future. Therefore, I realised that learning leadership cannot be complete without learning the life of the man who is not only the final Messenger of God but also the mercy for the whole of humankind. The life of Prophet Muhammad (PBUH) has not just taught us how to perform obligatory worships. He also demonstrated how to manifest the Divine message into our lives while wearing different hats at the same time: messenger of God, statesman, teacher, negotiator, social reformer, husband, father, grandfather, and even a warrior in the battlefield. He was a leader, a manager, and a strategist. His life is well explained by Hart (1989):

> "My choice of Muhammad to lead the list of the world's most influential persons may surprise some readers and may be questioned by others, but he is the only man in history who was supremely successful on both the religious and secular levels." (p.40).

Hart (1989) goes on saying: "We, see, then, that the Arab conquests of sevenths century have continued to play an important role in human history, down to the present day. It is this unparalleled combination of secular and religious influence, which I feel entitles Muhammad to be considered the most influential single figure in human history." (p.40).

Thus, Hart (1989) clearly explains that Muhammad (PBUH) was not only a spiritual leader but also a leader who can show the right direction in all aspects of our lives. My exploration into the Qur'an and the life of the messengers of God has transformed my understanding of leadership. On the other hand, my passion and exposure to these subjects helped me to understand the relevant teachings of the Qur'an, which in turn helped to find the answers to my questions related to leadership and strategy. Reading leadership literature alongside the Divine scripture put me on a quest to understand a kind of leadership that not only helps us to be successful in this temporary worldly life but also in the never-ending eternal life. This book is the result of this quest, which will set the scene for purposeful leadership. As you read through the pages, you will be inspired to dive into the mind-set of a purposeful leader who lives a life of significance by playing an essential role in creating a better family, a socially responsible organisation and a harmonious society while pursuing the grand mission to be successful in the eternal life. While discussing several leadership principles drawing upon the Divine scripture, this book will help you find answers to some of life's big questions:

1. Who are we?
2. Why are we created?
3. Who has created us and sent us here?
4. What is the significance of life?
5. Where is our final destination?
6. How is the success of our lives defined and measured?

Drawing on wisdom from the Divine scripture, this book transforms leadership thinking, inviting the readers on a journey to purposeful leadership, helping them to see life beyond death while formulating their success equation and developing their leadership style. Learning the art of living and bringing our purpose to life, call us to master the art of leadership and employ the right strategies and management techniques – not only to excel in our professional life but also in our entire life that encompasses everything we do. However, we cannot find the right course of our life to navigate into this complex and materialistic world unless we are absolutely clear about (a) the reality of life, (b) the definition of real and ultimate success, and (c) how these are linked to the purpose of life. Getting these strategic leadership issues wrong will lead to ultimate failure no matter how effective our strategies and how efficient our management techniques are.

This book aims to help you become an effective, purposeful leader while understanding the eternal life as a logical reality, and not just a matter of belief. I have talked to many people who have grand plans in their life. They are so organised that everything they want to achieve in the next ten, twenty, forty years, are on their vision boards. While talking to them, the one thing that I have not found on their vision board is the reality that they may die anytime, even in the next minute. They are ready with a robust plan – mostly with things that are uncertain i.e. things that may or may not happen. But they are not prepared for death, which is certain as every one of us will die but we do not know exactly when. Once I used to run a sales team in a company in London. There was a member of my team with whom I used to enjoy stimulating conversations on leadership, management, and strategy. It is fair to say that he was the best salesperson on the floor. I hardly had to coach him. Instead, there were occasions when I used to learn the art of selling from him. He often used to help me to coach other members of the team. We were very close friends and worked on various initiatives together. We also discussed the possibility of setting up a sales consultancy company. I can vividly remember that before leaving the office on a Friday evening, he came to me and said, "See you on Monday". On Monday, all the members of the team were present except him. We called his mobile number, but no one picked up the call. Afterward, when one of my colleagues called his number again, his brother picked up the call and informed us about the unexpected sad news: he died in his sleep. I heard the news, but my heart could not believe it until my eyes saw his dead body.

I could not live a normal life for a couple of months. I tried to understand why we are so concerned about this life, which can end at any time without any warning. What will matter then? How are our successes translated into eternal life? If we do not think and inquire about it, it is natural that we will not get the answer. My point is simple, although it may sound harsh.

Is there 'death' on your vision board?

We know when we were born, but we do not know when

we will die. Possibly, this is why we do not have 'death' in our plan. But in reality, death can overtake us anytime. I am not saying we should stop working and always think of death. What I am saying is to ask ourselves the questions:

1. Are we ready to meet our Lord?
2. Are we living by the directives of God?
3. Are we preparing for the judgment day when we all will have to stand before our Lord?

Contemplation and gaining clarity of these questions and designing a life accordingly can help us live a purposeful life where everything we do is aligned with the grand purpose of life. There are many advantages of thinking of death and the Day of Judgment, even from a leadership perspective.

1. It helps leaders to develop a long-term mindset and raises their sense of accountability to God.
2. This, in turn, positively influence the way they lead, shifting their focus from their own position and power to the rights of their followers.

Nonetheless, death, eternal life, or the Day of Judgment does not appear to have any place in the traditional leadership literature. This is the contribution of this book, which considers death, eternal life, the Day of Judgment, and our accountability to God while we serve others as a human and as a leader.

Although different traditions – western pioneered by Socrates, eastern exemplified by Confucius, and tribal propagated through proverbs – approach leadership differently (Adair, 2010), the traditional leadership literature deals with the theories of power, influence, and motivation. In the organizational context, the focus is mostly on the bottom line of the income statement.

Drawing on the work of Asrar-ul-Haq and Anwar (2018), let us briefly review the fundamental leadership definitions/ concepts before we introduce purposeful leadership (Table 1).

Table 1: The key focus of traditional leadership

Contributors	Conceptualisation of Leadership
Bennis and Nanus (1985)	Leadership is conceptualised as beauty, which can be known when seen but difficult to define.
Fiedler (1967)	Leadership is perceived as interpersonal relationship where power and influence is unevenly distributed to direct and control the behaviors of others.
Northouse (2009)	Leadership is viewed as power relationship existing between leaders and followers.
Wren, 1995	Leadership is viewed as effort of influencing through power to make subordinates submissive.
Conger and Kanungo, 1987; House, 1976	Leadership is defined as effort of influencing through power to transform the organization.

The traditional leadership theories are mainly concerned with how to influence people (mostly followers) to achieve worldly goals (in most cases) while remaining silent about eternal life and the achievement of hereafter goals.

Humphreys (2001) argues that leadership is an area of social science that is extensively studied but least understood. Northouse (2007) argues that the majority of the leadership definitions are related to the *trait, ability, skill, behavior, and relationship.* Although this dynamic discipline has evolved by moving from one fad to another (Yukl, 2010; Asrar-ul-Haq and Anwar, 2018), there are inadequate studies and scholarly works that incorporate the concept of death, eternal life, the Day of Judgment, and accountability to God while influencing the behaviour of the followers and helping them to be successful in the eternal life. Although the religious and faith leaders are inspiring people towards eternal life, there is very little literature on spiritual leadership as part of the mainstream leadership domain.

This book discusses a purposeful, faith-based leadership concept and views life beyond death when we all will have to stand for the final judgment of God for our individual actions as a human and as a leader. From the position of this book, God – our Creator – is at the center of the concept of purposeful leadership. The purposeful leaders are guided by faith in God and the grand purpose of life that God has assigned to His lieutenants (humankind) on earth. Their success depends on their ability to enable their people in designing a life where every action can be defined as either submission to God through direct invocation or via service to His creations i.e., good deeds (Amal–e–Sahleh) at the family, organisational and social level. I call it *"The Art"* of experiencing and manifesting a *"Lord–slave relationship"* while doing the usual worldly activities, where the Creator is the Lord and human beings are His slaves. This Lord–slave relationship ultimately frees human beings from all other kinds of slavery. Often we become a slave to our desires and spend our whole life chasing things such as the latest styles, luxury brands, expensive products, and so on. Without realising the fact, we also become slaves to many people in pursuing a worldly objective (e.g., oh, if he recommends me, I will surely get that job). This, directly or indirectly let us lose our dignity as a human.

Briefly, purposeful leadership starts by understanding why God has created us, and this has to come from the Divine scripture sent by God rather than other sources. While the traditional leadership focuses on our life within this world, the faith-based, purposeful leadership considers this world as a testing ground and focus on eternal life:

> He Who created death and life, that He may try which of you is best in deed: and He is the Exalted in Might, Oft-Forgiving; (Qur'an 67: 2)

In light of the above verse, as the worldly life is a testing ground, purposeful leaders do not disregard the importance of earthly life. Instead, they are more cautious in doing as many good deeds as possible and follow the commandment of God. They know that it is their deeds in this world that will decide their ultimate success and failure in eternal life.

Leadership is significantly essential for human beings, and it begins both at the individual and family level before going into the organizational and social level. In the Qur'an (66:6), Allah has called the believers to take the leadership role by asking them to save themselves and their families from the torment of the hellfire:

> "O you who believe! Save yourselves and your families from a fire whose fuel is men and stones, over which are (appointed) angels stern (and) severe, who flinch not (from executing) the commands they receive from Allah, but do (precisely) what they are commanded."

There is an implication of this verse both at the individual and family level. This verse signifies that every human being requires to assume the responsibilities to become a leader and save himself/herself and others under their influence such as the family members from the hellfire by leading a righteous life as prescribed by God and manifested by His last messenger, Prophet Muhammad (PBUH). In the

Qur'an (4:59), Allah also says:

> "O you who believe! Obey Allah, and obey the Messenger, and those charged with authority among you. If you differ in anything among yourselves, refer it to Allah and His Messenger, if you do believe in Allah and the last day; that is best, and most suitable for final determination."

In this verse, Allah commands the people to be loyal to their leader but if they differ with their leader on anything they should consult the Qur'an and the life of His Messenger. Thus, "The Divine Message" is the compass, which charts the course for the purposeful leaders, who believe in God and the Day of Judgement:

> This is the Book; in it is guidance sure, without doubt, to those who fear Allah. (Qur'an 2:2).

The teachings of Qur'an has been manifested through the life of the Prophet (PBUH). In a Hadith, Qatadah reported: I said, "O mother of the believers, tell me about the character of the Messenger of Allah, peace and blessings be upon him." Aisha said, "Have you not read the Quran?" I said, "O course!" Aisha said, "Verily, the character of the Prophet of Allah was the Quran." (Sahīh Muslim 746).

Remember, each one of you is a purposeful leader – at least for yourself and your family, no matter what your professional job title is. The real purposeful leaders are great followers – followers of God and His messengers. They are committed to growing through taking the helms of their lives, acquiring the Divine and the secular knowledge, and developing their character and values going through struggles of life.

Leadership is a quest, and we can learn it. We need to strive and go through different stages of hardships and challenges to become a purposeful leader. Chapter 2 will share some transformational stories and introduce a leadership compass with 12 transformational steps, divided into four quadrants: clarity, commitment, transformation and impact. Thereafter, the twelve transformational steps will be explained in detail in the following twelve chapters. The last chapter briefly summarises the essence of the twelve transformational steps with a focus on the importance of 'taking action' as no strategy will deliver any result if we do not take action to implement it.

> "There is a moment in every person's life when the awareness of their destiny bursts like a bubble onto the surface of their conscious mind. It is then that the weak avoid the realisation and busy themselves with the mundane tasks of their lives. It is also at that moment that the strong will awake and decide to take action to change their world for better and thereby secure themselves their rightful and valued place in the history of humankind." (Thompson, 1998, p.3).

Here are some questions for you to reflect before reading the next chapter.

1. In every one of our life, there are several transformational stories. These transformational stories have the power to shape our perception of leadership. An aha moment is when we capture them, reflect on then, learn from them, and when these stories inspire us to set us on a journey to purposeful transformational leadership. Could you capture any transformational stories of your life? What are those? How these stories have shaped the way you perceive and understand leadership? Write a 1000-word transformational story of your life.

2. Why the clarity of the grand purpose of life is critical to the study of leadership?

3. What is the fundamental difference between the concepts of traditional leadership and leadership that perceives life beyond death while considering our accountability to God on the Day of Judgment?

I believe this book will help you embark on a journey of self-discovery that offers clarity of purpose, growth through lifelong learning, transformation through overcoming adversity, and how to make a personal impact on this world as God's lieutenant.

So, with the leadership compass, presented in this book, enjoy your leadership journey. The world is waiting for you to make an impact:

Find your purpose, bring it to life, and leave a legacy.

THE LEADERSHIP COMPASS
12 Transformational Steps

There was no better time than now to become a leader and influence others with the power of your idea. There was a time when title and position might have some advantage to access to a large number of people and influence them. However, in the age of digitization and social media, if you have a powerful message, you can access to anyone in the world – and influence and inspire them. In their book, "No Ordinary Disruption: The Four Global Forces Breaking All the Trends", Manyika, Woetzel and Dobbs (2016) identified some interesting findings: to access to 50 million people, radio took 38 years, TV 13 years, iPod 4 years, Internet 3 years, Facebook 1 year, and Twitter only 9 months.

Due to the advancement of science and technology and the proliferation of social media in all aspects of our lives, there was no better time to inspire others. To become a leader, you do not need to come from a well-known family, an Ivy League school, or a Russel Group University. Science and social media have broken the barriers to information channels. It is now the power of your message that counts. It is the purpose, potential, and principles that matter. It is your vision and values, character, and conduct that determine whether people will entrust you to lead them.

If you have a big dream to become a purposeful leader who will stand for a purpose, who will lead with character and uncompromising integrity, I have excellent news for you. There is hardly any competition! There are many leaders, but only a few of them demonstrate strong character. There are many leaders, but only a few of them believe that they are accountable to God and behave accordingly. In recent times, the world has witnessed plays after plays performed by 'characters' in leadership position one after another, who demonstrate everything but not the character. Munroe (2014) has given a vivid narration of this play:

> "In the dynamic drama of contemporary leadership playing on the world stage today, there are many "characters" who lack character. Moreover, the trail of history is littered with many would-be great men and women who harnessed the reins of power in various fields – political, social, economic, corporate, athletic, spiritual, and more. The

wielded great influence and/ or control over the lives of others; many felt the weight of material wealth and fame – only to have it all disintegrate and blow away like dust in the wind because of their tragic deficiencies of character." (p.1)

There are many leaders, but there are very few who put God first, their people second, and themselves last. To serve others (and eventually become a leader), you neither need a title nor a corner office.

- We all can start serving humanity and contribute to make this world a better place.
- We can start by picking up a banana skin from the road to save another person from slipping.
- We can help an elderly person on the street who needs little support and attention.
- We can even sacrifice (or at least share) our lunch with a homeless person. We can also spare some of our free time, and a small portion of our income to support a more significant cause through charity work.

We need to stop waiting and start at some point. This is crucially important. Many leaders often lead without any title and make tremendous contributions to help others in numerous ways. Still, we hardly know them and recognize their contributions. They do not do it for recognition; instead, their calling drives them. They do not do it for running for the president or for a promotion to get into the corner office. They do not even do it for followers on social media. They serve others to get a sense of fulfillment. They are unsung heroes who work silently. We should put spotlights on them, and spread their stories to inspire others.

CONNECTING THE DOTS

In my quest to develop a leadership compass that can help us embark on a transformational journey to unleash our leadership potential, I looked back to my life. I have faced and overcome many setbacks, sufferings, and challenges throughout my life. Along the way, I have received support from many unsung heroes. I have also reflected on the books and other leadership literature I have read. To connect the dots, I was inspired by the famous quotation of Steve Jobs to look back instead of looking forward.

> "You can't connect the dots looking forward; you can only connect them looking backwards. So you have to trust that the dots will somehow connect in your future. You have to trust in something — your gut, destiny, life, karma, whatever. This approach has never let me down, and it has made all the difference in my life." Steve Jobs

As I looked back, I can recollect that I came across the concept of leadership while reading a Bengali poem when I was a Year VII student. My science teacher, Muhammad Motiar Rahman, who was a great reciter of Bengali poems, inspired me in reciting. He not only inspired me to be a reciter but also trained me on different occasions with his personal care and affections. When I was shortlisted to attend a National-level

Recitation Competition, he brought me to Dhaka, the capital of Bangladesh, so that I could attend the competition. The affection, support, and personal care that I have received from my school teacher, Motiar Rahman, can never be forgotten and paid back. He was one of the very few people who could see some potentials in me. He played a significant role in developing confidence in me when I desperately needed it.

Later on in my life, this had encouraged me to take several challenges. One of the biggest challenges was to leave the Navy voluntarily in the middle of my career, setting my sail for uncertainties. The poem that embarked me on a transformational journey was about a voyage of a valiant sailor into the rough sea during a stormy night who survived in all adversities through faith in God, courage, and perseverance. I have already mentioned it in chapter 1. Therefore, I learned that a leader should have at least three attributes: faith, courage, and perseverance. Then throughout my career in the Navy whenever I came across extremely rough sea and stormy weather, this poem was a source of inspiration. However, my perception of leadership kept on transforming throughout my service in the Navy. Each training I had attended at home and abroad and each book I had read shaped my leadership thinking in some ways. A number of my colleagues whom I worked for and worked with have influenced the way I view leadership today. I also learned from the naval job itself. The life on-board ships, the time spent at sea, working as part of a team at sea and shore – all these experiences taught me invaluable lessons about life and leadership. Some of these lessons are as follows:

> a. No matter how talented, efficient, and hardworking we are, a team always achieves more than its members can achieve individually.
>
> b. Reading helps, but the real leaders are developed at work while testing their knowledge in real-life scenarios. However, to go into the next level, there is no short-cut to reading and learning. This means there are two aspects of leadership: Knowing and being. While reading and finding a coach can be excellent sources of knowing leadership, being a leader happens at work.
>
> c. Before you become a leader, you need to learn to be a follower and find a mentor.
>
> d. The quality of your leadership depends on the character, substance, and integrity and not on your charisma, style, and image. Leaders are positive change-makers and not celebrities. Leaders are developed through the sacrifice of blood and sweat.

I was lucky to work with many people from different industries who displayed exemplary leadership attributes. Eventually, many of them became my mentors. When I was doing my cadet training in the naval academy, I was influenced by the work ethic and leadership of *Lieutenant Abu Ashraf and Lieutenant Maksumul Hakim*. Both of them were my divisional officers, and my values were drawn from the principles they demonstrated. Soon they became my role models. Now, one of them is a Rear Admiral, and the other is a Commodore. Both of them were outstanding officers and known to everyone for their professionalism and dedication to naval service. One of them was very pious and regular in his prayers, which particularly fascinated me. During my initial days, they were my inspiration, and when I had thought about leaders, their names used to come to my mind.

I attended my midshipman training onboard an HMS Jaguar Class Frigate that was commissioned in Bangladesh Navy in 1978. This training changed me into a different person. I am convinced that the Navy is not just a profession but a school of leadership: teaching leadership for life. My values were further developed during my watch-keeping training onboard the first missile frigate of the Bangladesh Navy. The commanding officer of the ship, named *Commander Bazlur Rahman*, was well-known in the Navy for his charismatic leadership style, and I was thrilled when I got my joining letter to serve under his command. I was personally influenced by his boldness and spirituality. He is the only Commanding Officer whom I have seen leading prayer while the ship was at sea. He also had a reputation for having uncompromising honesty, which inspired me. He always demanded a very high standard from his officers. Initially, I was nervous about working around him. I vividly remember that once he was conducting a watch-keeping examination for our senior batch during a sea trip while I was working as the Assistant Officer of the Watch. I heard him telling the candidates that if they could work like me, they would qualify the exam. This inspired me a lot, and I could have completed my watch-keeping in the following three months. The Commanding Officer also gave me several assignments, which helped me develop my leadership skills. Now, Bazlur Rahman is a Rear Admiral, enjoying his retired life.

I was also appointed as the Assistant Missile Officer of the ship, which created an opportunity to work closely with the Missile Officer, *Lt M Musa*. He was another outstanding officer trained in the Malaysian Navy. He was exceptionally thorough in his work with sound professional knowledge. He was possibly the most likable officer in the frigate. For any professional inquiry, he was my first port of call. His spirituality, courage, and straightforwardness also inspired me to choose him as a role model. He was extremely humble with exceptional capability to work with people and inspire them. I had worked long hours with him – every moment was an opportunity for me to learn. After my watch-keeping, when I was posted to other ships and establishments, I did not have a chance to work with him again, but we cherished our memories whenever we had the opportunity to meet. His merit found him at the Royal

College of Defence Studies (RCDS) at Kings College London as a Captain. I could see his passion for education when I met him in London during his RCDS course. Returning from Kings, he was promoted to the rank of Commodore, but his quest for formal education did not stop. He completed his MPhil. Recently he got another promotion and became a Rear Admiral in the Navy. He has also submitted his PhD thesis.

Another officer who has helped in my leadership development was the newly joined Executive Officer (XO) of the ship, *Lt Commander M A Islam*. He was possibly the youngest XO of a frigate at that time. I was already trained by him when I was a midshipman. He was very inspiring for being a hands-on leader who likes to experiment. One thing that I noticed in him was his interest in statistics. He knew how to use statistics in favour of his argument and was very logical in his pitch. He was mostly driven by statistics rather than assumptions while speaking and making decisions. After joining the ship, he launched a new venture of developing a non-skid weather deck to improve safety. He could persuade the Commanding Officer with his idea. He then united the whole ship's company in delivering it. In a week, the ship's weather deck changed. Because of our previous working relationships, he started to hand me over a lot of tasks. This also helped me to develop my skills and professional knowledge. A few years later, on a stormy night, we encounter a cyclone while entering harbor onboard a patrol craft. By the time, he became a Commander. He never left the bridge and supported us. The Executive Officer, *Lt Mustaque Ahmed* and I were present were also present in the bridge until we came to a safe place and anchored the ship. Although I was the navigating officer, during this crucial moment, Lt Mustaque and Commander Anwar displayed an exceptional sense of responsibility and the commitment to the service. We were extremely alert as the ship was passing through the shallow water and we were encountering poor visibility and extreme wind. I was not only doing my job but also watching these two officers and was fascinated by their calmness and professionalism during real emergencies. One thing I learned that night was how to stay calm in an emergency and how to inspire the whole team to deliver their best when needed. Finally, we managed to bring the ship out of danger. It was a valuable experience for me to learn ship-handling in inclement weather and the art of teamwork. Lt Mustaque is now a Commodore in the Navy, and Commander Anwar is enjoying his leave pending retirement as a Rear Admiral.

A few months later, I faced a similar situation, returning through the same channel on another stormy night. This night my course-mate, *Lt Arif Ahmed Mustafa*, was onboard on temporary duty. He was present in the bridge throughout the passage to help me. Truth to be told: I possibly could not complete the task in the same way without his wholehearted support on that night. There was one particular incident when one of his immediate wheel orders saved us from an unwanted situation of hitting a buoy that was not visible due to rough sea. I had the opportunity to witness how calm he was during the crisis, which is expected from the leaders. Recently, Arif has been promoted to the rank of Commodore, but there is no change in his lifestyle. Although he is holding one of the most important appointments in the Navy, planning the careers of the sailors, he is still a humble and dedicated person like a Lieutenant I had seen when I was in the Navy. Indeed, he is living with his family in Lieutenant's residence even though he is a Commodore. Recently, during a conversation with him, I wanted to know about his experience of bringing a Large Patrol Craft from China. His vivid description of the voyage straightened my hair.

I could see a bonafide leader in front of me. His stories covered adversities after adversities, and they are multifarious. One thing caught my attention when he said that he had experienced one of the verses of the Qur'an during this voyage: "To Him belong the ships with raised sails, sailing through the seas like mountains." (Qur'an 55: 24). Arif told me clearly: there was no reason he could have saved the ship given the adversities he and his team faced, without the mercy of God. He had to make decisions and change them very often based on the situation. He made 4-hour sea watch into 2-hour so that people can somehow survive on the work posts against the mountainous waves that kept hitting the ship. He said that leaders should adapt to the changing situation and their professional knowledge and skills are very important to develop a team who can face any challenge. One thing he highlighted was about learning: "Leaders should seek every opportunity to learn their profession well." Arif was humble to accept that his expertise and success came not from his talents but because of his hard work, dedication and eagerness to learn.

My perception of leadership kept on transforming after I willingly retired from the Navy to explore life on dry land, where I learned that starting a new career in a new country could be as challenging as surviving military training. The struggles of beginning from scratch with my wife and two little sons on the same lifeboat tested our character developed in the Navy and helped us solidify our moral values. Faith and prayer kept on guiding me onto the right course. This is the time I started reading the biographies of business leaders and top management, leadership, and strategy books. Several authors who further shaped my thinking are Michael Porter, Jim Collins, John Maxwell, Bill George, and Simon Sinek. After I completed my MBA from the University of Strathclyde and was looking for jobs in the UK, I became interested in business leaders. Steve Jobs was one of the leaders who inspired me the most.

While working in the UK financial services sector, I came across *Andy Pearce*. Andy is currently the CEO of an insurance company. However, when I met him first, he was managing the operation of a well-known brand of a big global insurance company. Andy used to talk to me whenever there was an opportunity despite his higher position in the company. He liked my quest for a PhD while on a full-time job. When he knew that I was interested in business leadership, and my first book was published, he became my mentor. We used to have an hour session every month. I was really amazed to see his humility. I could not imagine that a leader running a half-billion-dollar business would spare an hour of his time every month to discuss various management, leadership, and business strategy. He opened his heart and shared many stories of his life with me. These include his successes and failures and how he learned from these incidents. Andy was a people-centric leader, used to give everyone a chance to talk. He learned it from his father, who always encouraged him to put forward his opinion on any collective family decision. Usually, he was invited to put forward his opinion on any crucial matter over a family meal. So, being an eight-year-old child Andy became a part of the decision-making club of the family and practiced the same in his own life. I found an incredible similarity between his father and my father when he told the stories. We used to have meals together, and my father used to ask similar questions. Andy says: "When I tell my wife and children that their opinions count, they all contribute to family decision-making. When I ask the same thing to my team members at work, they contribute towards the company decisions."

I learned from Andy that to energize and mobilize people, we need to allow them to be part of the decision-making process. Although, today, Andy is a successful leader who knows the art of connecting with his people and creates a climate where people feel being part of an engaged team, his initial journey to leadership was not rosy. Often he became emotional while talking about his journey, and we end up forming a trusting relationship. Later on, my elder son was fascinated by a statement made by Andy during his visit to our home. While he was entering into our small flat, my son was anxious if he could find himself comfortable. Andy replied: "I have come to see the person and not the place." That day we had another enthusiastic conversations with Andy on leadership and management, and my elder son joined as well.

My leadership thinking was further transformed after I had met another man. In 2013, I joined a university as a part-time lecturer to teach several modules in the areas of marketing and strategy. While teaching a strategy module, I met Jonathan Groucutt. Jonathan was the Module Leader for strategy. Initially, I was a bit nervous as I had never taught at the university before. On the very first day, Jonathan spared an hour to meet me and explained everything about the module. He was friendly and supportive. I left with a feeling that I know him for ages. He continued to support me. As a result, being new in the industry, I did not face any problem. The support he provided was far beyond the scope of his job responsibility. Soon I noticed that he was equally helpful to all members of the team. Jonathan is a published author with tons of experience in the UK higher education sector providing strategic guidance to institutions. He became an authority in his field. He was very keen to share his knowledge, experience, and skills to develop others, no matter whether they are part of his team or not.

While adopting myself in the UK higher education sector, I was looking for a person who could help me as a mentor. The initial meeting with Jonathan opened an opportunity. My first working session with Jonathan is still evident in my mind when I attended a benchmarking meeting led by him. I was not clear about the rubric and the way of checking quality in assessment. However, Jonathan ran a benchmarking session with detailed procedures and briefs. He went through each paper so thoroughly that I became very confident about the whole process in just one session. Being in the Navy, I had a feeling that my sense of work ethics should be second to none. However, attending the first benchmarking meeting with Jonathan, my perception changed. Jonathan's standard was exemplary. His comments on each paper were at least four times more than anyone of us attended the meeting. As a newly joined academic, I made the optimum use of Jonathan's knowledge and experience and was always keen to learn from him. Then surprising every one of us, one day, Jonathan went on voluntary retirement. I sensed that Jonathan was responding to his personal calling but was not sure of it. But when our Head of Department left with a new job, the senior management team of the university requested Jonathan to come back and help them hire a new Head for the department. Jonathan came back and started to lead our department. This again created an opportunity for me to work with him. My joy knows no bounds.

Then I worked with Jonathan even more closely when he led the team in developing a new academic programme. This was a completely new experience for me. Jonathan has an egalitarian leadership style, which inspired us to go extra miles. His knowledge, experience, and expertise easily won our trust and confidence in his leadership style. End of the day, it was a transformational experience for me, and I kept on taking Jonathan's advice to improve my research and writing. One thing for which Jonathan will never be forgotten is his support to help others grow. I found this is a fundamental requirement for someone to be a leader. A leader must create a climate where people can learn and grow. His support did not stop even after he left the university after the newly hired Head of the Department joined. Now that Jonathan is not working in the same university, but he is still supporting me as a mentor. Jonathan is my first port of call when I face any intellectual challenge. He is also helping several other colleagues, supporting them in their personal development. Recently, someone has become an external examiner. During a meeting, she had been talking about Jonathan's contribution towards preparing her for this. Now, Jonathan is leading and supporting people without a job title. He is not concerned about salary or further promotion and doing everything selflessly. I can see his selfless leadership style has helped me develop some values, finding reasons to lead. Here are what I learned about leadership while working with Jonathan.

Leadership is a self-effacing calling to help others to grow. To serve others, you do not need a title or a contractual relationship with them. And, possibly, the best way we can help others is by sacrificing our time and sharing our knowledge and experience. The real success of leadership is to make an impact by helping others to become leaders, not followers. If all leaders focus on this, there will be a chain impact, and society will see more leaders.

Self-effacing calling to help others is a powerful inner force that can set one on a leadership development journey. While talking about his internal motivation, one of my colleagues, *Ben Botes,* said that he found his inner calling while working for a charity. Triggered by a feeling that part of being human is supporting others in need, his service to humanity started in 1990 when he was a student at the University of South Africa. Several initiatives to support local charities in Cape Town inspired him to join the movement. Since then, he has been part of many efforts under the banner of several charities to help children in crisis from different backgrounds, and restore and empower traumatised communities so they can realise their full potential. He started as a telephone counselor, working a few nights per week. Currently, he is supporting them in fundraising for their work across Africa. Most of the charity he is supporting operates in the areas with a high crime rate, where the lack of employment and high drug dependency rate leads to more crime and a high death rate amongst youths. These charities and foundations are providing job creation, community uplifting through entrepreneurship, agriculture, peacebuilding initiatives, and trauma therapy to the communities where they operate. Ben sees his inner motivation to support the communities and projects in South Africa as a way of giving back. There is no feeling better than being part of a movement that feeds 300 poor kids every day, providing food and nutrition to those who need it. Talking to Ben, I learned a compelling calling of giving back should drive leadership.

While reflecting on my experience of working people from different backgrounds, I felt I could connect the dot and was ready to develop my leadership compass.

Initially the three significant dots that came to my mind were *commitment, transformation, and impact*. We must commit to become a leader and grow through continuous learning. As the journey to leadership is not rosy, we need to transform ourselves going through struggles and overcoming adversities. Then also need to make an impact in the world, and for that, we do not always need to do great jobs as many of us may not have that opportunity, but we need to do our jobs with great care and love. Here, Steve Jobs always had an influence on me.

> "You've got to find what you love. And that is as true for your work as it is for your lovers. Your work is going to fill a large part of your life, and the only way to be truly satisfied is to do what you believe is great work. And the only way to do great work is to love what you do. If you haven't found it yet, keep looking. Don't settle. As with all matters of the heart, you'll know when you find it. And, like any great relationship, it just gets better and better as the years roll on. So keep looking until you find it. Don't settle." Steve Jobs

I could have found tremendous love in my work, not only when I was in the Navy but also in my current job involving research, teaching, and learning. What inspired me most is the opportunity to teach my students coming from many parts of the world but also learn a lot from them. Possibly, I learned more from my students than I taught them. In fact, I believe that we need to change the way we teach in the modern-day, particularly if we want to develop our students as tomorrow's leaders. *We need to teach them the study of leadership rather than leadership itself.* Learning how to study a subject invites the students on lifelong learning so that their education does not stop when they graduate. Thus, teaching the tools and techniques of learning is the rule of the games of teaching in the modern-day when knowledge is a commodity but can be powerful if we can transform it into wisdom and insight.

Let us come back to the leadership compass that I was trying to develop. I was not entirely happy with the one that I had conceptualised. I kept on reviewing the three dots – commitment, transformation, impact – again and again. I could feel there was at least one more dot missing. But I was not quite sure of it. I could figure out this when I turned my focus from leadership literature to the Divine scripture. What I learned is neither human beings came into this world by accident, nor had God created the heaven and the earth and everything in between playfully.

> "Not for (idle) sport did We create the heavens and the earth and all that is between!" (Qur'an 21:16)

I also realized that a leadership compass giving direction to purposeful leaders cannot be developed without understanding the purpose of life. However, in search of the purpose of life, we most often ask the wrong question – *"Why am I here?"* – as if we have descended on earth by ourselves or we have created us by ourselves. Indeed, it is maker (manufacturer) rather than the equipment itself that decides what a piece of equipment can do. Likewise, the purpose of our life is determined by our Creator and not by us. So, the right question to ask is: *Why am I created?* While exploring the Divine scripture, I discovered that human beings are given special honour to be God's lieutenants (vicegerents) on earth, and they have a grand purpose. In the Qur'an, Allah says:

> Behold, thy Lord said to the angels: "I will create a vicegerent on earth." They said: "Wilt Thou place therein one who will make mischief therein and shed blood? - whilst we do celebrate Thy praises and glorify Thy holy (name)?" He said: "I know what ye know not." (Qur'an 2:30)

Finally, I could find the missing dot of my leadership compass, which I believe to be the most essential cornerstone of purposeful leadership. It is the "clarity" – clarity of why we are created. So, the leadership compass (Figure 2.1) is ready to be unfolded with a hope to set you on a transformational journey to becoming a purposeful leader in 12 steps. Are you prepared to set your sail? Let's cast-off.

Figure 1: The Leadership Compass

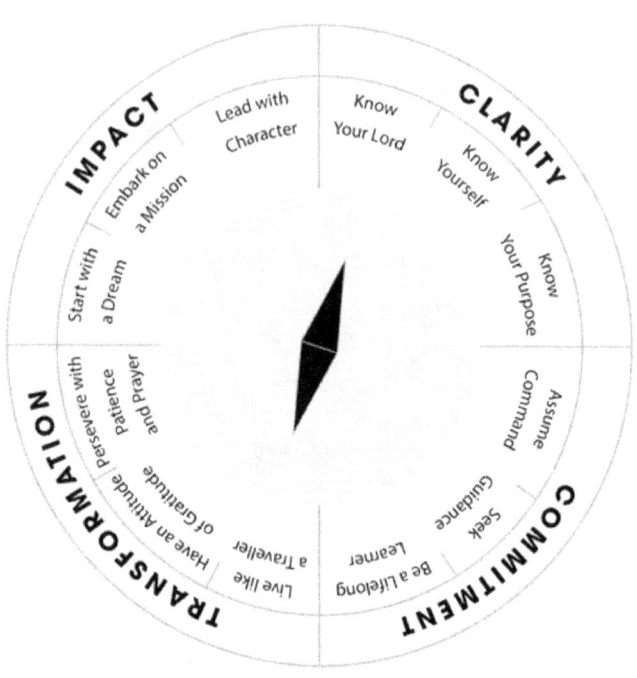

Copyright © 2020 S M A Moin

I. CLARITY

The first quadrant of the leadership compass is 'clarity,' which is grounded from the domain of theosophy that intersects the areas of theology and philosophy. Getting into a leadership journey without knowing our role on earth, i.e., the fundamental reasons we are created and sent on earth, is like embarking on a ship without knowing its port of call. If leaders themselves do not understand why they are living in this world, how can they show the direction to others? However, we cannot know why we are created until we know who has created us and who we really are.

1. Know Your Lord: Put God First

The main question is not "what is the purpose of our life?" instead, "who decides the purpose of our life?" That's a great beginning to find our origin and establish our relationship with our Creator. If we do not learn to ask the right question, even a correct answer will not help us to find the right direction. Thus, knowing our Lord is one of the starting points of this compass. The purposeful leaders not only know their Lord but also put God first.

2. Know Yourself: Meet God's Lieutenant

Knowing who, indeed, you are as a human will open up an excellent way for you to serve humanity and make a difference in the world. An essential question to start with the quest to discover your identity from a multidimensional angle is, "Who am I?" The sooner we know the answer, the sooner we are prepared to find out the purpose of our life and our crucial role on earth. This will lead to both self-awareness as well as self-awakening, which will set a purposeful leader to reclaim his identity.

3. Know Your Purpose: Set Your Moral Gyro

Mark Twain said, "You have two important days in your life. The day you were born, and the day you know why." However, if you contemplate deeply, I believe, you will realize that the most momentous day in your life is the day you discover the reason you are created - in other words, the grand mission you are assigned with by your Creator. Knowing our purpose gives us a sense of clarity about life. Life without clarity of purpose can be termed as "existing" rather than "living." You need to embark on a journey to seeking the meaning of life, rather than escaping from life's grand mission. You need to learn to talk to your soul and be true to yourself. Imagine, if this is the last day of your life, what would you do? How would you like the world to remember you? If you have clarity about the purpose of your life, every single day will set you on a mission. You are here to submit to your Lord and serve humanity (Moin, 2019), and you cannot do it without knowing your purpose.

II. COMMITMENT

The second quadrant of our leadership compass is 'commitment', grounded from the domain leadership, management, and personal development. Here, we define commitment as the firm conviction to grow by taking full responsibility for our life, continually seeking the guidance of God, and being a lifelong learner.

4. Assume Command of Your Ship: Take the Helm of Your Life

You can get someone to do the push-ups for you, but it is not going to build your muscles. You are the captain of your ship (life). If you do not assume the command of your lifeboat, someone else will. How can you take responsibility for others if you don't take responsibility for your own life?

5. Seek Guidance: Find Freedom through Faith

Faith in God gives us the power to step forward without even seeing any light at the end of the tunnel. God provides guidance to those who sincerely seek it and ponder upon His creations. Thus, it is essential that as God's lieutenants, we continually seek His guidance. The guidance of God brings us from darkness to light. Faith in God finds hope in despair, and the courage and patience to move on. Dependence in God finds us ease in hardship no matter how difficult our situations are, we know we have someone to return to, we know God is watching that we are trying our best.

6. Be a Lifelong Learner: Develop the Third Eye

In the Qur'an (2: 31-32), Allah has mentioned that human beings are learning creatures, and God is their teacher (Moin, 2019), and "those who know" and "those who don't know" are not equal (Qur'an 39: 9). It is the knowledge that can help us come out from darkness to light, which includes both the divine wisdom that helps us understand our Lord and His creations and secular knowledge that has been taught by the pen(Qur'an 96: 1-4). Learning is not limited to obtaining a degree or graduating from university. It is a lifelong quest. The beauty of educating ourselves is to discover how little we know. Knowledge gives us confidence; wisdom saves us from arrogance. And having a curious mind with an open heart can help us to embark on lifelong learning.

III. TRANSFORMATION

The third quadrant of the leadership compass is transformation – transformation through struggles. This is also supported by the theories of leadership development. When I was a naval cadet, I came across a saying, "Train hard, fight easy," which is also popular in the Army, Air Force, and Marine. All the Messengers of God, who are the greatest leaders of all times, have gone through periods of struggles. The whole life of Prophet Muhammad (PBUH) was full of struggles. The day he died, there was no fuel in his home to put on the lamp.

7. Live Like a Traveller: Find Abundance in Less

Life on earth is a journey. Having a traveler mindset lets us experience abundance in less. The realization that we are just travellers on earth for a short period helps leaders to focus on their grand mission instead of being distracted by the materialistic world.

8. Have an Attitude of Gratitude: Focus Your Eyes on the Prize

Life is full of countless blessings, but it takes an attitude of gratitude to count them. Happiness is in the art of noticing what we "do have" rather than what we "don't have." Developing an attitude of gratitude and focusing the eyes on the enormous prizes we are already living with, helps leaders to stay positive during the time of hardships. And if the leaders do not remain positive during the crisis, how will the people they lead?

9. Persevere with Patience and Prayer: Transform through Struggles

Human beings grow through suffering. Our real character is revealed when we are tested. We are not made by our circumstances but by how we respond to them. Perseverance, patience, and prayer make us overcome any test of life, and take us nearer to our Creator. In the Qur'an (2:155), Allah has mentioned that He will test us with fear and hunger, loss of goods or lives or fruits of toil, and has given glad tidings to those who patiently persevere.

IV. IMPACT

The fourth quadrant of the leadership compass is impact, and when you are in this quadrant during your leadership development journey, you are already a leader. The most celebrated American CEO of the 20th Century, Jack Welch said, "Before you are a leader, success is all about growing yourself. When you become a leader, success is all about growing others." (Welch and Welch, 2005). Thus, when you become a leader, you need to make an impact in the world, and the first impact you can do, in the words of Jack Welch, is to help others grow. This is the level when you need to inspire your people through your dream, vision, and mission and lead them by your character and values that you have developed in the other quadrants. We know about some of the great leaders who have made tremendous contributions in this world through their mission, vision, and character.

10. Start with a Dream: Navigate with a Vision

A leader is a dreamer. They not only dream of a better future for the people they lead but also use their dreams to inspire their followers. Great leaders also know how to turn their 'dreams' into 'a vision.' Indeed their 'vision' is so clear that people can see it even before it becomes a reality. It is the vision that helps leaders to take their people on-board and navigate them with a greater sense of purpose.

11. Embark on a Mission: Make Service Part of Every Day

While leading with a vision, great leaders set a mission to mobilize their people. One of the greatest missions every leader should bring to life is serving humanity and uplift the world by their crafts and businesses! Prophet Muhammad (PBUH) said: "On a journey, the leader of a people is their servant."

12. Lead with Character: Bring Values to Life

Some leaders fail to earn the trust of their people as they are more pre-occupied with their egos, vanity, and charisma rather than developing a robust set of values and principles that define their moral character. Eventually, leaders' moral character determines what they are allowed to do and what they are not. While our values and principles define our character, our character defines us. We don't need to be perfect, but we need to have the moral character to stand against injustice and evil. A leader with character can be tough enough to count a wrong as wrong even everyone supports it.

A leader with character treats a right as right even everyone is against it. However, they are humble, and they try to pursue their people with the beauty of their character. The pious and purposeful leaders make them accountable to their Lord (God) as they know God is watching their actions, and they are answerable during the Day of Judgement.

They are concerned with the rights of their people instead of their power and authority. The leader with the best character is the last and final Messenger of God, Prophet Muhammad (PBUH). While describing his character, Allah says in the Qur'an:

> "And thou (standest) on an exalted standard of character."
> (Quran 68:4)

Now, it is your time to reflect. I found "reflection" to be one of the best ways of self-discovery. Are there people in your life who inspire you? What have you learned from them? Have you read any leadership book that has triggered your inner passion? Have you implemented the knowledge you gained from these books in your life? Reflect on your answers and make a developmental plan for the next six to twelve months. Remember, there is a vast difference between knowing leadership and becoming a leader by putting your knowledge into practice. However, knowing is a useful step to start the journey.

PART I

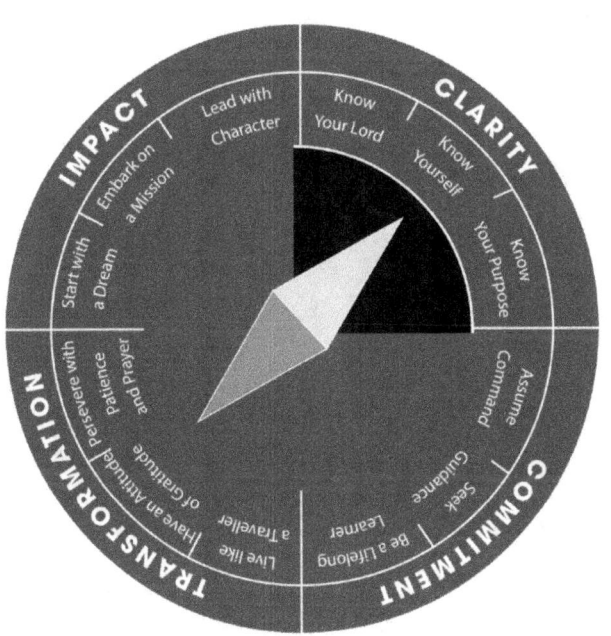

CLARITY

Say: He is Allah, the One and Only;
Allah, the Eternal, Absolute;
He begets not, nor is He begotten;
And there is none like unto Him.

(Qur'an 112: 1-4)

1

KNOW YOUR LORD
Put God First

The most important day of your life is not the day you were born, but the day you know why. However, you cannot genuinely understand why you are born until you discover who has created you and the reason for His creation. Like the scientists decide the purpose for the things (i.e., robots, machines, toys, etc.) they create, the purpose (i.e., the primary reason you are here) of your life is decided by your Creator, who is also the Creator of the whole universe. Thus, the purpose is not something you invent – it is something that is assigned to you, and you discover.

Rethinking leadership through Divine teachings inspires human beings to have clarity about the purpose of their lives. This involves discovering who you are, Who has created you, why He has created you and sent you on planet earth, where you are going, what is the significance of your life, and how your success is measured.

Many people may not be comfortable with these questions. I have tried to discuss these questions with many leaders, and they did not like my initiative. However, if you put some time aside and think seriously, I believe you will appreciate that these are some of the most critical questions in our life.

To find the answers to these questions, you need to use both head and heart in finding the truth. In our quest to know our Lord, we can go deeper and deeper, but in this chapter, I will briefly discuss Who our Creator is drawing on the teachings of the Qur'an, which is believed by about 1.8 billion people to be the final Devine scripture. The rest of the questions will be answered in the next two chapters.

In no way, the explanation of this chapter will be comprehensive in conceptualising our Creator. I will also request you to read the tafsir of the Qur'an. You will find plenty of literature that you can also read alongside this chapter. However, for those who are not very clear about how our Creator introduces Himself in the Qur'an, I will use a three-dimensional model (Figure 3.1). I believe this will make a reasonable start and will give you a foundation for further research. Our Creator (who is our Lord and God of the universe) can be conceptualised in three ways:

1. By a Qur'anic definition that sets four criteria to understand Who our God is.
2. By the beautiful names of God that explain His attributes.
3. By the cosmological signs that we can see around us if we pay our curious attention. Allah mentions: *"Behold! in the creation of the heavens and the earth, and the alternation of night and day,- there are indeed Signs for men of understanding,-"* (Qur'an 3:190)

Figure 3.1: Three-dimensional Model to Conceptualise God

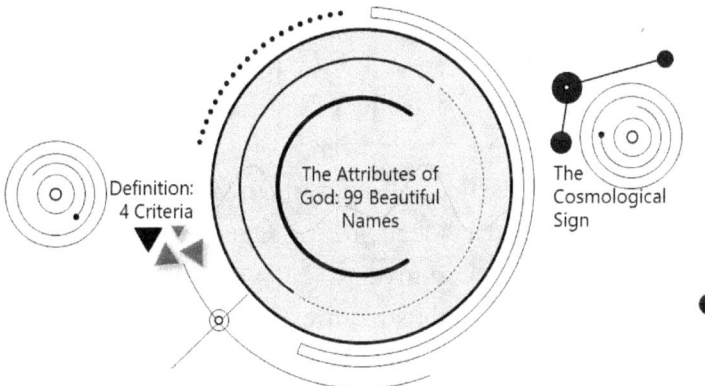

THE FOUR-CRITERION DEFINITION OF GOD

According to Islamic scholars, Surah Al-Ikhlasa (Qur'an 112: 1-4) gives a 4-criterion definition of God. This is known as the touchstone of God, which determines Who the real God is.

Clarity 53

> Say: He is Allah, the One and Only;
> Allah, the Eternal, Absolute;
> He begets not, nor is He begotten;
> And there is none like unto Him.

This is a four-line Surah, and each line represents one Criterion.

Criterion 1: Say: He is Allah, the One and Only

Criterion 1 clearly mentions that God is "One and Only". This signifies the Oneness of God. 'One and Only' is different from 'One.' One (1) can be 2, 3, or 4 by adding with another 1, 2, and 3, respectively. However, 'One and Only' points only to 'One'. It can be logically deduced that for the smooth functioning of the universe, as the Creator and Controller of this universe, God has to be 'One and Only'. The existence of more than one God would create conflicts. Besides, the nature also provides the cosmological evidence of the Oneness of God. The grand design of the universe that we can observe and experience all-around us manifests the Oneness of God. There is significant consistency in the design of everything in the universe. This perfect and consistent design of the world easily substantiates that the supreme designer of the universe and everything in it is one. A signature at the bottom of the artwork can help us to recognize the artist. Likewise, the similarity in the design of everything in the universe (e.g., lands, jungles, trees, mountains, deserts, rivers, oceans, sky, etc.) provides logical proof that One Great Designer has designed this whole universe. He is none but God: One and Only. In the Qur'an, Allah inspires human beings to look at the sky and find any defect in His creation, if they can.

> He Who created the seven heavens one above another: no want of proportion will you see in the creation of (Allah) Most Gracious. So turn your vision again: see you any flaw? Again turn your vision a second time: (your) vision will come back to you dull and discomfited, in a state worn out. (Qur'an 67: 3-4)

If we look at the universe, we cannot find any defect in the creation of God. This was echoed by the word of the greatest scientist, Einstein:

> "Try and penetrate with our limited means the secrets of nature and you will find that, behind all the discernible concatenations, there remains something subtle, intangible and inexplicable. Veneration for this force beyond anything that we can comprehend is my religion. To that extent I am, in point of fact, religious." (Jammer, 1999, p. 39-40)

Einstein's words also promote the beauty of the craftsmanship of nature and the existence of supernatural power. Many of us accept this supernatural power as God, Who is the 'One and Only.' The perfect 'designs' of nature and the consistency in the cosmological signs are enough to feel the existence of the Creator. The swirling pattern of "Golden Spiral" is an example of the consistent design pattern: "snail's shell, the shape of galaxies, the swirling formation of hurricanes, flowers and even fingerprints" (Zakariya, 2015, p.14). Due to the advancement of scientific research, we now know about the exceptional consistency of anticlockwise rotation of things in the universe:

1. The anticlockwise rotation of the moon around the earth.
2. The anticlockwise rotation of the planets of the solar system, including the earth around the sun.
3. The anticlockwise orbit of the sun along with the whole solar system around the galaxy.
4. The anticlockwise orbit of the galaxies in space.
5. The anticlockwise flow of blood in our body.
6. The anticlockwise motion of an electron in an atom.
7. The anticlockwise rotation of low-pressure on land or at sea.

Interestingly, this anti-clockwise rotation is also consistent with the Tawaf around the Kaba by the Muslims during Hajj and Umrah. The Qur'an (21:33) states that *"It is He Who created the night and the day, and the sun and the moon: all (the celestial bodies) swim along, each in its rounded course."* Another example of the consistency in the creation can be noticed in the design of human beings: the shapes, sizes, positions, and proportions of the various parts of the human body. Are they not designed perfectly? Could you think of human having five eyes, six hands, thirty fingers, seven legs, and so on? What about their location being different? We know that different people look different, but their fundamental design remains unchanged. The differences simply show their exclusivity. Now, as you ponder on the design of human beings, read the following verse of the Qur'an.

> But He fashioned him in due proportion, and breathed into him something of His spirit. And He gave you (the faculties of) hearing and sight and feeling (and understanding): little thanks do you give! (Qur'an 32: 9)

Here, Allah says that He has designed human being in due proportion. There are many verses in the Qur'an like this. If we use our cognitive faculty and ponder, we can feel the existence of 'One and Only' designer of the universe, and He is God. Another example of the consistency of design is DNA. DNA contains the general information associated with all living creatures.

> "Even though living things may outwardly appear to be different, at the generic level, because of their shared creator, they can be very similar. For example, as humans we share approximately 50 per cent of our DNA with banana trees. We find that the DNA, the blueprint, is shared by all living things across nature. This common design points to a common designer – One Creator behind it all." (Zakariya, 2015, p.14 -15).

Criterion 2: Allah, the Eternal, Absolute

The second criterion (Allah, the Eternal, Absolute) means that Allah (God) is self-sufficient and everlasting. He is complete with His own virtues. He does not need anyone's help but everyone needs Him. This criterion also means that Allah cannot die. Many people believe that God can die and resurrect. This criterion dismisses this possibility. If Allah dies, who is in charge, controlling the universe in the absence of Him?

Drawing on the analogy that nothing comes out of nothing and nothing is created automatically, some people ask: Who has created God? This criterion, along with the third and fourth criterion, addresses that question: God is uncreated, which is evident in the Quran:

> He is the first and the last, the evident and the hidden: and He has full knowledge of all things. (Qur'an 57:3)

Criterion 3: He begets not, nor was He begotten

The third criterion means God does not have any parents and nor any begotten child. He is entirely free from all the properties that are attributable to His creations. Being the Highest and the Most Holy, associating activities that are relevant to His creations does not honour God. Instead, this is a severe humiliation to His status. We need to think carefully before making any comment about the Creator of the universe. There are many verses in the Qur'an that warn humankind regarding this.

> To Him is due the primal origin of the heavens and the earth: how can He have a son when He has no consort? He created all things, and He has full knowledge of all things. (Qur'an 6:101)

Criterion 4: And there is none like unto Him

The fourth criterion signifies the uniqueness of God that He cannot be compared with anyone or anything. This also reinforces the first (Say: He is Allah, the One and Only) and third (He begets not, nor is He begotten) criteria. Had God could be begotten, He could have been compared to all those creations who beget and are begotten.

> [He] who made for you the earth a bed [spread out] and the sky a ceiling and sent down from the sky, rain and brought forth thereby fruits as provision for you. So do not attribute to God equals while you know [that there is nothing similar to Him] (Qur'an 2:22).

This verse first shows God's enormous mercy upon us; and then warns us not to compare Him with anyone else. We must recognise Who our Creator is before we can understand why has He created us and sent us into this universe.

In summary, Surah Al-Ikhlas gives a definition of God using four criteria, which distinguish Him from His creations and everything else. The other verse of the Qur'an (Verse 255 of Surah Al-Baqarah, also known as Ayat-ul-Kursi: The Verse of Throne) gives us an understanding of the dominion of His throne and power.

- Allah - there is no deity except Him, the Ever-Living, the Sustainer of [all] existence.
- Neither drowsiness overtakes Him nor sleep.

- To Him belongs whatever is in the heavens and whatever is on the earth.
- Who is it that can intercede with Him except by His permission?
- He knows what is [presently] before them and what will be after them, and they encompass not a thing of His knowledge except for what He wills.
- His Kursi extends over the heavens and the earth, and their preservation tires Him not.
- And He is the Highest, the Greatest.

Pondering upon various elements of this verse will also help us understand the greatness and uniqueness of our Lord Who is the Creator of the heaven and the earth.

THE BEAUTIFUL NAMES OF GOD AND THEIR SIGNIFICANCE

We can also conceptualise our Creator through His beautiful names. In the Qur'an, a total of 99 names of God have been mentioned. These are known as Al Asma Ul Husna: The Beautiful Names.

> And to Allah belong the best names, so invoke Him by them… (Qur'an 7:180)
>
> Allah – there is no deity except Him. To Him belong the best names. (Qur'an 20:8)
>
> He is Allah, the Creator, the Inventor, the Fashioner; to Him belong the best names. (Qur'an 59:24)

These names explain God's attributes, characteristics and virtue and effective way of conceptualising Him as we cannot see God in the worldly life. However, the Qur'an confirms that those who will pass the test of this world and will enter into heaven will have the special reward of seeing their Creator.

> Some faces, that day, will beam (in brightness and beauty) – Looking towards their Lord; (Qur'an 75: 22-23)

A number of His names are mentioned in Surah Al-Hashr.

> Allah is He, than Whom there is no other god – Who knows (all things) both secret and open; He, Most Gracious, Most Merciful. Allah is He, than Whom there is no other god – the Sovereign, the Holy One, the Source of Peace (and Perfection), the Guardian of faith, the Preserver of Safety, the Exalted in Might, the Irresistible, the Supreme: Glory to Allah. (High is He) above the partners they attribute to Him. He is Allah, the Creator, the Evolver, the Bestower of forms (or Colours). To Him belong the Most beautiful names: whatever is in the heavens and on earth, does declare His praises and glory: and He is the Exalted in Might, the Wise. (Qur'an 59: 22-24)

Out of 99 names, we can see that the following fourteen names of Allah are mentioned in the last three verses of Surah Al-Hashr.

> Ar Rahman (The Most Gracious)
> Ar Raheem (The Most Merciful)
> Al Malik (The King)
> Al Quddus (The Most Holy)
> As Salam (The Ultimate Provider of Peace)
> Al Mu'min (The Guardian of Faith)
> Al Muhaymin (The Guardian, the Preserver)

Al Aziz (The Almighty, the Self Sufficient)
Al Jabbaar (The Compeller)
Al Mutakabbir (The Dominant one)
Al Khaaliq (The Creator)
Al Baari (The Maker)
Al Musawwir (The Fashioner of Forms)
Al Halim (The Forbearer, The Indulgent)

According to Islamic scholars, these names can be categorised into two main groups: Jamal (Attributes of Beauty) and Jalal (Attributes of Majesty).

Al Asma Ul Husna – Jamal

The names under the category of Jamal (Beauty) inspire us to acquire good qualities as we are the creations of God. For example, as God is merciful and compassionate and we are representing God as his vicegerent (will be explained in the next chapter), we also need to be kind to His creations: fellow human beings and other creatures. Allah encourages human beings to illuminate and beautify their inner selves with the qualities of their Lord.

> (We take our) colour from Allah, and who is better than Allah at colouring. We are His worshippers. (Qur'an 2:138)

Al Asma Ul Husna – Jalal

The names under the category of Jalal (Majesty) help us to realise and experience the God-slave relationships

(Servitude): "It is You we worship and You we ask for help." (Qur'an 1:5). These names that come under both Jamal and Jalal let us call our Lord during prayers and while seeking His help.

> And to Allah belong the best names, so invoke Him by them. (Qur'an 7:180).
>
> Say: I seek refuge with the Lord and Cherisher of Mankind, The King (or Ruler) of Mankind (Qur'an 114: 1-2)
>
> [Who say], 'Our Lord, let not our hearts deviate after You have guided us and grant us from Yourself mercy. Indeed, You are the Bestower. (Qur'an 3:8)

The prayer of Prophet Abraham mentioned in the Qur'an is an excellent example for us to contemplate.

> And [mention] when Abraham was raising the foundations of the House and [with him] Ishmael, [saying], 'Our Lord, accept [this] from us. Indeed You are the Hearing, the Knowing. Our Lord, and make us Muslims [in submission] to You and from our descendants a Muslim nation [in submission] to You. And show us our rites and accept our repentance. Indeed, You are the Accepting of repentance, the Merciful. Our Lord, and send among them a messenger from themselves who will recite to them Your verses and teach them the Book and wisdom and purify them. Indeed, You are the Exalted in Might, the Wise.' (Qur'an 2:127-129)

THE SIGNIFICANCE OF THE NAME: ALLAH

In the opening Surah of the Qur'an, the name 'Allah' is used to introduce God. This is the name that has also been used in Surah Al-Ikhlas, which gives the definition of God. Allah is the proper name of God, whereas the other 99 names explain His attributes and virtue. The name 'Allah' manifests the essence of Monotheism. The tradition of belief in many Gods (Polytheism) assumes that each God has some particular attribute. In other words, different Gods with different attributes need to coordinate to accomplish a task (e.g., creating the universe or smoothly running its operations). In doing so, Gods need to either compromise or involve in conflict with each other. The concept of different gods having different attributes, limits the power of God. The doctrine of Monotheism centres on the belief of the "The One and Only God". He possesses all the attributes of the Self-sufficient and Eternal Master. The significance of the name Allah suggests that all these attributes are associated with Him. Therefore, Allah is the name that encompasses all the attributes expressed through the rest of the 99 names. To know and understand more about our Creator and the Lord of the heavens and the earth, you can read my book, The Purpose of Life: Understanding the Divine Message through the lens of Leadership and Strategy. In this book, I have explained the concept of God in detail and divided them into three chapters.

LEADERSHIP IMPLICATION

Knowing about God has profound implication in the way we develop ourselves as leaders and eventually the way we lead. It enables us to know the supreme Lord of the universe, Who has created everything. It allows us to gain clarity about our origin. How can we know about ourselves if we do not know who created us? All leaders are entrusted with some responsibilities, and they need absolute clarity about who they are accountable to, saving them from reckless behaviour. Acquiring the knowledge of God and developing God-consciousness give leaders a sense of accountability to their Creator. This also reinforces their responsibilities for their people and accountability to them. Understanding the significance of the names of God (Jamal) enables leaders to develop the values and qualities expected out of them as the vicegerent of God.

On the other hand, understanding of the names of God (Jalal) will make leaders humble, enabling them to experience the Lord-slave relationship. This will inspire them to find *meaning* in the service of their people.

Behold, your Lord said to the angels: "I will create a vicegerent on earth." They said: "Will you place therein one who will make mischief therein and shed blood? – whilst we do celebrate Your praises and glorify Your holy (name)?" He said: "I know what you know not."

(Qur'an 2:30)

2

KNOW YOURSELF
Meet God's Lieutenant

At some stages of our lives, many of us want to know who we are. Before we can lead others, we need to lead ourselves. And we cannot lead ourselves if we do not know who we are. Self-awareness is a crucial step in leadership development. Before we can become a leader, we need to know who we are. It is also critical to understand our role on earth. However, in this chapter, I want to let you discover your identity, focusing on your relationships with your Creator. This is a simple logic that our Creator is the One Who can really tell who we are. If you are not convinced, just ask a simple question: who calls a TV a TV? Is it the TV or the scientist, who created it? Understanding "who we are" is the second step in seeking clarity in our leadership compass. And to know our identity from the perspective of our Creator, we need to turn ourselves to the Divine scripture.

RECLAIM YOUR IDENTITY

Let us now know the genesis of the creation of human beings that God has revealed in the Qur'an. I believe it will help every one of us to reclaim our identity.

God's Lieutenant

In the Qur'an (Surah Al–Baqarah, verse 30 to 39), it is clearly mentioned that human beings were created with a purpose by God[1]. From the words of God, we know that human beings were created as God's lieutenants (vicegerents) on earth.

> Behold, your Lord said to the angels: "I will create a vicegerent on earth." They said: "Will you place therein one who will make mischief therein and shed blood? – whilst we do celebrate Your praises and glorify Your holy (name)?" He said: "I know what you know not." (Qur'an 2:30).

Thus, the job of humankind is to obey the commandments of God. We will reveal this, leading to the discovery of the purpose of life in the next chapter.

---

[1] Tafsir of Ibn Katsir; and the thematic analysis of Surah Al-Baquarah by Shaykh Muhammad al-Ghazali (Shamis, 2005)

Intellect, Free Will, and Strategic Choice

The subsequent verses also unveil that "Human beings are learning creatures, and God is their teacher" (Moin, 2019, p. 84). What differentiates Adam (PBUH), the first human, from other creations of God is the power of knowledge.

> And He taught Adam the names of all things; then He placed them before the angels, and said: "Tell me the names of these if you are right." They said: "Glory to You, of knowledge We have none, save what You have taught us: In truth it is You who are perfect in knowledge and wisdom." He said: "O Adam! Tell them their names." When he had told them, Allah said: "Did I not tell you that I know the secrets of heaven and earth, and I know what you reveal and what you conceal?" (Qur'an 2: 31-33)

Thus, human beings, as God's lieutenants on earth, are blessed with intellect and free will that entitles them to make choices: decide between right and wrong. They can follow the commands of God. These verses offer two "strategic choices" for human beings to select one from.

1. They can either be humble and obedient like angels (who consistently celebrating the praises of God and glorifying His holy names) and be successful.
2. Or, they can be arrogant and proud like Iblis (Satan) and fail to achieve the object of life.

Recognising the Enemy

Another important thing that the story of Adam (PBUH)

unveiled is the identification of the direct enemy of humankind. The Qur'an clearly mentions that the greatest enemy of human beings is Iblis (Satan). Iblis is so jealous of human beings that he did not hesitate to refuse when God commanded him to prostrate to Adam (PBUH).

> And behold, We said to the angels: "Bow down to Adam" and they bowed down: not so Iblis: he refused and was haughty: he was of those who reject faith. (Qur'an 2:34)

Life on Earth: For a Short Term and Test

Then God commanded Adam (PBUH) and his wife to live in heaven and enjoy the blessings of his Lord. God gave them some instructions, but Iblis out of his jealousy, deceived them and made them slip.

> We said: "O Adam! Dwell you and your wife in the garden; and eat of the bountiful things therein as (where and when) you will; but approach not this tree, or you run into harm and transgression." Then did Satan make them slip from the (garden), and get them out of the state (of felicity) in which they had been. We said: "Get you down, all (you people), with enmity between yourselves. On earth will be your dwelling-place and your means of livelihood - for a time."(Qur'an 2: 35-36)

According to the verses mentioned above, life in this world is for a term. No one can deny this fact. Whether we like to think about death or not, none of us is going to live in this world forever. Indeed, humankind has been sent into this world for a very short-term. During this time, they are tested. In other words, the world is a testing ground.

> Be sure we shall test you with something of fear and hunger, some loss in goods or lives or the fruits (of your toil), but give glad tidings to those who patiently persevere, Who say, when afflicted with calamity: "To Allah We belong, and to Him is our return": They are those on whom (descend) blessings from Allah, and mercy, and they are the ones that receive guidance. (Qur'an 2:155 -157)

Mistakes and Repentance

In the mistake of Adam (PBUH), there is a lesson for human beings. Human beings are curious and susceptible to errors. If they are not mindful and careful, Iblis can easily deceive them. Because Iblis is the direct enemy of human beings, his only job is to deceive them so that they disobey the guidance of God and go astray. Iblis wants human beings to be disobedient like him, so they too fail to achieve the purpose of life.

> Then learnt Adam from his Lord words of inspiration, and his Lord turned towards him; for He is Oft-Returning, Most Merciful. We said: "Get you down all from here; and if, as is sure, there comes to you guidance from me, whosoever follows My guidance, on them shall be no fear, nor shall they grieve. "But those who reject faith and belie Our signs, they shall be companions of the fire; they shall remain in it." (Qur'an 2: 37 – 39).

These verses also explain that although human beings are

susceptible to error, they can seek repentance of their Creator as God is merciful and oft-forgiving. To qualify in the test of life on earth, human beings need to follow the guidance of their Lord sent through His messengers. And the last and final Divine scripture (the guidance for the whole of mankind and jinn kind) is the Qur'an, revealed upon the last and final Prophet Muhammad (PBUH).

> Praise be to Allah, Who has sent to His servant the book, and has allowed therein no crookedness: (He has made it) straight (and clear) in order that He may warn (the godless) of a terrible punishment from Him, and that He may give glad tidings to the believers who work righteous deeds, that they shall have a goodly reward, In which they shall remain for ever: (Qur'an 18: 1-3)

In summary, we must remember that we are God's lieutenant on earth and three things - intellect, free will and choice – differentiates us from other living creations of God.

THREE DIMENSIONS OF HUMANKIND

So far, we have briefly discovered our identity as the God's Lieutenants on earth (e.g. Khalifa: The Qur'anic word) which also establishes our relationships with our Creator (e.g. Khaliq or Al–Khaliq: The Qur'anic word). The leadership significance of this implies that every human being is a leader (Khalifa: God's Lieutenant) with the responsibility to manifest the grand purpose given to them by their Creator (Al–Khaliq). This perception is drawn from the teachings the Divine Scripture. Becoming a genuine God's Lieutenant (Khalifa) is a lifelong quest; and from that perspective, purposeful leadership is also a lifelong quest. This is why I have used the phrase *"12 steps to becoming a purposeful leader"* rather than *"12 steps to become a purposeful leader"*. However, as humankind is made of body, mind and soul, it requires an understanding of at least three dimensions: The physical-self, the intellectual-shelf and the spiritual-self.

The Physical Dimension

Physical dimension relates to the physical body of the human being. The human body is a gift from our Lord, and it is our moral duty to lead a life that keeps us healthy and active. Controlling the way of eating and drinking, doing regular exercise and leading a healthy routine is essential for leaders. Leaders are slaves of God and servants of their people. They need to stay fit with loads of energy to (1) submit to their Lord through worship, and (2) serve their people. The state of our physical-self also impacts our other dimensions. In fact, the obligatory worships are designed to bring human being into a disciplined life, which contribute to our physical and mental health.

The Intellectual Dimension

In this book, I conceptualise intellectual dimension as our ability to use intellect that differentiates humankind from other creations. "And He taught Adam the names of all things…" (Qur'an 2:31) shows what an incredible power God has given human beings with the ability to think: use critical reasoning. In other words, this is the power of human minds. But, the crucial question remains: where does our mind reside? There is the body of research that suggests that using of intellect is one of the three functions of the soul:

> **Cognitive:** The use of our intellect.
>
> **Affective:** When linked to heart (Qalb), enabling us to experience emotion, feeling, anger, joys and so on, and seek the guidance of God.
>
> **Conative:** Includes our behaviour, attitude, response to things happen to us.

It is difficult to establish a clear line between our intellectual and spiritual dimensions. I will not even make an attempt to do so. What is important is we need to grow by nourishing our body, mind and soul and develop a righteous heart. Prophet Ibrahim (PBUH) prayed to God, so the He grants him a sound heart (righteous heart) that only matters on the Day of Judgment (Qur'an 26: 83-89).

> 83. "O my Lord! bestow wisdom on me, and join me with the righteous;
> 84. "Grant me honourable mention on the tongue of truth among the latest (generations);
> 85. "Make me one of the inheritors of the Garden of Bliss;

86. "Forgive my father, for that he is among those astray;
87. "And let me not be in disgrace on the Day when (men) will be raised up;-
88. "The Day whereon neither wealth nor sons will avail,
89. "But only he (will prosper) that brings to Allah a sound heart;

The Spiritual Dimension

A profound understanding of "Yourself" is not complete without understanding the concept of the soul that explains our spiritual dimension. I must admit that I am not an expert on the topic of soul, but my discussion will only give you some pointers so that you can conduct further research. To understand our complete-self, we need to understand the concept of three terms mentioned in the Quran, which are Nafs, Rooh and Qalb. The Qur'anic terms, Rooh and Nafs have been translated as the soul (Jawaid, 2010). Often Rooh is translated as both (1) soul and (2) spirit, and Nafs has been translated as (1) soul and (2) self or our (3) own self. Qalb is the heart but related to spiritual heart and not the physical heart. The Qur'an considers the human being as the presence of soul (Nafs and Rooh) inside the body.

Rooh (Sprit/Soul)

The Quran defines Ar-Rooh as the order of Allah, which happens instantaneously, and not perceptible and beyond the scope of science (Jawaid, 2010). In the Qur'an, Allah has also mentioned that He has given very little knowledge to human beings about the Rooh.

> They ask you concerning the spirit (of inspiration). Say: "The spirit (comes) by command of my Lord: of knowledge it is only a little that is communicated to you, (O men!)" (Qur'an 17:85)

The Qur'an also uses the term Rooh in two primary contexts. First, Rooh as Holy Sprit (Rooh Al Quds) that refer to angels Angel Jibraeel (Rooh-ul-Ameen: Jawaid, 2010).

> Say, the Holy Spirit has brought the revelation from thy Lord in truth, in order to strengthen those who believe, and as a guide and glad tidings to Muslims. (Qur'an 16:102)

Jawaid (2010) vows that because their primary function is to implement the commands of Allah, the term Rooh is used to indicate angels, particularly Jibraeel. Second, Rooh refers to Divine Energy (Sprit of His Command) and further conceptualised into two categories.

> (1) Divine energy manifested as a command (Rooh Min Amr)
>
> He does send down His angels with inspiration of His command, to such of His servants as He pleases, (saying): "Warn (man) that there is no god but I: so do your duty unto Me." (Qur'an 16:2)
>
> (2) Divine energy breathed to form life endowing it with certain faculties (Min Rooh)
>
> But He fashioned him in due proportion, and breathed into him something of His spirit. And He gave you (the faculties of) hearing and sight and feeling (and understanding): little thanks do ye give! (Qur'an 32:9)

Nafs (Self/ Soul)

Drawing on extensive research on Qur'anic verses on the Nafs and Rooh and relevant literature, Jawaid (2010) goes on to explain that Nafs (meaning Soul here) was exerted in the human body by the command of Allah. According to Qur'an, this means during our sleep, Allah extracts our Nafs from our body. Again we wake up when our Nafs is returned our body by Allah. We die in sleep when the Nafs is held up. When the Nafs permanently extracted from our body, we die.

The Qur'an has mentioned about three main kinds of Soul/Self (Nafs): (1) Nafs-e-Ammarah (*The Inciting Nafs*), (2) Nafs-e-Lawwamah (*Self-accusing Nafs*) and (3) Nafs-e-Mutmainnah (*Nafs at Peace*).

Nafs-e-Ammarah

Nafs-e-Ammarah refers to Inciting Nafs or the Evil-prone Soul. When a soul enters into a human body, it is uncorrupted but is prone to evil (Jawaid, 2010), known as Nafs-e-Ammarah (The Inciting Nafs).

> "Nor do I absolve my own self (of blame): the (human) soul is certainly prone to evil, unless my Lord do bestow His mercy: but surely my Lord is Oft- forgiving, Most Merciful." (Qur'an 12:53)

This soul is prone to evil can be compared to the *'evil desire' or inclination to do what has been forbidden by our Lord.* Thus, restraining from the unlawful desire of the *Nafs-e-Ammarah* through the God-consciousness is the real test of the human being. As the direct enemy of humankind, out of jealousy, Satan (Iblis) can whisper to the Nafs of the humankind.

> Then began Satan to whisper suggestions to them, bringing openly before their minds all their shame that was hidden from them (before): he said: "Your Lord only forbade you this tree, lest you should become angels or such beings as live for ever." (Qur'an 7:20)

While humankind has been given free will to choose either good and the bad, to safeguard their Nafs from evil desire and to keep its commitment, it is guided by conscience and revealed books. The evil-prone soul can respond in two ways (Jawaid, 2010): (1) Either, excels itself by warding off evil desires using intellect and God-consciousness; (2) Or, degrades itself by following its evil desires, and become a corrupt soul.

> And its enlightenment as to its wrong and its right;- Truly he succeeds that purifies it, And he fails that corrupts it! (Qur'an 91: 8-10)

Nafs-e-Lawwamah

Nafs-e-Lawwamah refers to Self-accusing Nafs or Evil-conscious Soul. It is the soul that is conscious of evil and has a tendency to accuse oneself when commits a sin. This soul sometimes lets someone commit a sin but then starts feeling guilty, remorse, regretful, and embarrassment. The guilt increases so much that person repents, seeks forgiveness to Lord, and comes back. While fighting a battle with the trials, tribulations, temptations of bodily desire, greed and love of worldly things, this soul can avoid evil most of the time. However, often choose to respond to evil desires (hawa) while failing to use conscience but tries to correct the future behaviour seeking Allah's grace and pardon after repentance.

Say: "O my servants who have transgressed against their souls! Despair not of the mercy of Allah: for Allah forgives all sins: for He is Oft-Forgiving, Most Merciful. (Qur'an 39:53)

Nafs-e-Mutmainnah

Nafs-e-Mutmainnah refers to *Nafs at Peace or The Satisfied Soul*. The soul continually strives to remain conscious of evil and try to improve its behaviour. Due to their endeavour, it develops a second nature of doing right and disliking wrong. The soul, through aligning itself with the will of Allah, finds happiness and satisfaction in the worship of Allah. Eventually, it becomes a satisfied soul (Nafs-e-Mutmainnah).

> (To the righteous soul will be said:) "O (you) soul, in (complete) rest and satisfaction! "Come back thou to your Lord,- well pleased (thyself), and well-pleasing unto Him! ""Enter you, then, among My devotees! "Yea, enter you My heaven! (Qur'an 89:27-30)

While differentiating between Rooh and Nafs Jawaid (2010) vows that pre-existing soul (Nafs) is connected to the human body by the order (Rooh) emanating from Allah through a process of breathing (Nafakha). To be successful both in this world and in the hereafter, leaders need to focus on developing a sound and righteous "Spiritual Heart" (Qalb), where the faith (Iman) of the believers resides and which receives the guidance of God.

> Many are the Jinns and men we have made for Hell: They have hearts (qloob) wherewith they understand (yafqahoon) not, eyes ('ayn) wherewith they see (yubseroon) not, and ears (azaan) wherewith they hear (yasmaoon) not. They are like cattle,- nay more misguided: for they are heedless (of warning) (ghafeloon). (Qur'an 7: 179)

> Do they not travel through the land, so that their hearts (and minds) (qloob) may thus learn wisdom (ya'qeloon) and their ears (aazdhan) may thus learn to hear (sam'a)? Truly it is not their eyes (absar) that are blind ('ama), but their hearts (qloob) which are in their breasts (as-sodoor). Qur'an 22: 46)

Jawadin (2019), says the following:

"While we see the external world through our eyes ('ayn), it is only by processing these information in the brain that we develop foresight (basara). Similarly we hear things around us through our ears (aazaan), but only by processing these information in the brain that we decide what to pay attention to (sama'a). The Quran tells us that just like the information we collect through our eyes and ears help us develop foresight and heedfulness, the information we collect through our heart (qalb), under the breast (sadr),a help us learn wisdom (ya'qeloon) and develop understanding (yafqahoon)." (p.2)

CASE STUDY

Many leaders develop their values from their families, which further reinforced by the way they learn and grow later in their career. In fact, leaders continue to learn from different credible sources, including the environment they come from. Our families, friends, societies, and countries are also schools of life. The story of one of my naval colleges, Abdullah Al Maksus, is worth sharing. Both Abdullah and I joined the Navy together in 1990. In fact, we also attended the same inter-services selection board. This was a 4-day intensive process, testing candidates' IQ, EQ, psychological, behavioural and leadership capabilities. Abdullah has a reputation of being a leader who consistently strives to take his leadership into the next level. I met him after 12 years in 2017 and had an enjoyable thought-provoking conversation.

It was just about a year, Abdullah returned to Bangladesh after completing his secondment at the UN Headquarters in New York. He was a Planning Officer (P-4) in the military wing, doing strategic and operational planning of UN peacekeeping missions. He received a medal from the UN Secretary-General for his exceptional service. When talking to him, I could sense his passion for authentic leadership. I was interested to know the number one priority of his leadership agenda. His answer was short and straightforward: team building. He tried his best to infuse in his people a sense of pride of serving the nation, dignity and self-respect. In fact, the moment we deeply realise that we are God's Lieutenant on earth – representing Him and accountable to him – we are more encouraged to display ethical values and behaviour. Abdullah goes on saying that he desperately promoted a sense of responsibility and team spirit, putting the team's interest before the individual's own. He also encouraged every member of the ship, sharing their personal experiences while he shared his own: this promoted belongingness and mutual trust. I asked him about the sources of the values that he bring to his professional and personal life. I found him a bit of emotional while answering this question.

> My parents and grandparents laid the foundation of my values, which further reinforced by the Divine teachings.

Raising in a joint family helped him learn several values that are invaluable to leadership, which further reinforced by his dedicated reading and research of the Divine scripture. Abdullah is a Captain now and doing the National Defence College. He has a very colourful career with command, staff duties and teaching and learning experience that has contributed to his transformation. Abdullah's story teaches us that we all are the architect of our career – our actions define who we become and how we serve others as a leader.

LEADERSHIP IMPLICATION

The Divine scripture gives everyone of us an identity – the Lieutenant (Khalifa in Arabic) of God while the God is the Creator (al-Khaliq in Arabic) of this universe. Thus, all of us are leaders with the accountability to our Creator. We need to develop ourselves in three dimensions: body, mind and soul to experience our physical, intellectual and spiritual transformation. This will help us grow as leaders with a long-term mindset – life beyond death. Purposeful leaders align leadership with the grand purpose of life. Their focus should be to develop a righteous "Spiritual Heart" (Qalb) that Prophet Ibrahim (PBUH) pursued to Allah through his prayer (Qur'an 26:89).

Were they created of nothing, or were they themselves the creators?

(Qur'an 52: 35)

3

KNOW YOUR PURPOSE
Set Your Moral Gyro

While working in the warships, one of the things that changed my perception of leadership and life was *true north*. The metaphorical meaning of *'true north'* has a position in leadership (George and Sims, 2007). Usually, about four to five hours before a ship casts off, the gyro is started to settle onto the true north. A sailor's life is inextricably connected with a compass and the true north. True north is the reference point for a gyrocompass that sailors use to finds the directions at sea, helping them to steer the intended course.

As a compass should know its true north to give the right directions at sea, every one of us should find our true north to chart the right course of our life. Do you know what the leaders' true north is? Leaders' *true north* is their purpose, which guides them. When leaders gain clarity of their purpose and can communicate it clearly, people can relate to it. For example, when Martin Luther King Jr. delivered his *'I have a dream'* speech, people from all walks of America came to listen to his address. There was no internet or social media to make the event viral. Despite the limited media coverage, people turned out to support the purpose that Dr King stood for. He called for a fair and just American society without any discrimination. People who came to listen to him also wanted to live in a society where everyone is treated equally. They too dreamed a nation where people are judged based on their character - not by the colour of their skin. Purpose gives leaders the basis to hold on. It sets their moral gyro and continually provides them with a line between what they can and cannot do – *a line that differentiates good from the bad.*

The purpose of life is also like the North Star that helps us find the direction so that we can reach our destination. Nonetheless, we come across many kinds of purpose. Every organisation we work for has a purpose. Every job role has a purpose. The purpose of a teacher is not the same as the purpose of a firefighter. The purpose of a lawyer is not the same as the purpose of a janitor. Each job has a unique role. So, these micro purposes can better be coined as "role" rather than "purpose". In this chapter,

I am not interested in the role. Instead, my focus is on the grand purpose of life. To be more precise, the why of our life: why were we created and sent to this universe? This is possibly the most crucial question we have as Mark Twain reminds us: "You have two important days in your life. The day you were born and the day you know why." To answer this question, we need to go back to the Divine scripture again as the question – why we were created – can only be answered by our Creator.

In the last two chapters, we have discovered who our Creator is; who we are; and our relationship with our Creator. This chapter is dedicated to revealing the grand purpose of life assigned by our Creator. Getting it wrong means we will fail to achieve the objective of living. There is no reason to believe that human beings were created without a purpose.

To lead successfully, leaders must understand the purpose of their life. It is not pleasant to know, it is an imperative. Otherwise, they may be able to lead their people to accomplish a task or a mission, but they will not be able to help them to achieve the ultimate objective of life. Leading without knowing the grand purpose of life, limits the effectiveness and role of a leader, narrowing it down to particular areas only. However, mainstream leadership literature does not cover the purpose of life that is assigned by our Creator. Indeed, every one of us is responsible for knowing the true meaning of life. Thus, you are liable to find out why you were created. You will face the consequences for the choice you make. I asked myself this question, and I am satisfied with the answers I have found. I can share my experience with you, but I want you to find the solutions for yourself if you are not happy with my answer. This reminds me of the story of Prophet Ibrahim (PBUH). In search of God, the approach he took thousands of years before really moved me. Here are few verses from the Qur'an about Prophet Ibrahim's (PBUH) conversation with His father that God has revealed in the Qur'an for the humankind to ponder:

> Behold, he said to his father: "O my father! why worship that which hear not and see not, and can profit you nothing? "O my father! to me has come knowledge which has not reached you: so follow me: I will guide you to a way that is even and straight. "O my father! serve not Satan: for Satan is a rebel against (Allah) Most Gracious. "O my father! I fear lest a penalty afflict you from (Allah) Most Gracious, so that you become to Satan a friend." (The father) replied: "Do you hate my gods, O Abraham? If you forbear not, I will indeed stone you: Now get away from me for a good long while!" Abraham said: "Peace be on you: I will pray to my Lord for your forgiveness: for He is to me Most Gracious. "And I will turn away from you (all) and from those whom you invoke besides Allah. I will call on my Lord: perhaps, by my prayer to my Lord, I shall be not unblest." When he had turned away from them and from those whom they worshipped besides Allah, We bestowed on him Isaac and Jacob, and each one of them We made a prophet. And We bestowed of Our mercy on them, and We granted them lofty honour on the tongue of truth. (Qur'an 19: 42–50)

This shows how keen Prophet Ibrahim (PBUH) was in his endeavour to find the true God. The rewards from God was phenomenal. All the prophets after him came through his lineage. This special honour given to him was mentioned in the Qur'an, Bible and Torah. The following verses show the wisdom of Prophet Ibrahim (PBUH) in confronting with the unbelievers and people who do not believe their Creator as their One and Only God.

> When the night covered him over, he saw a star: he said: "This is my Lord." But when it set, he said: "I love not those that set". When he saw the moon rising in splendour, he said: "This is my Lord." But when the moon set, he said: "unless my Lord guide me, I shall surely be among those who go astray". When he saw the sun rising in splendour, he said: "This is my Lord; this is the greatest (of all)". But when the sun set, he said: "O my people! I am indeed free from your (guilt) of giving partners to Allah. "For me, I have set my face, firmly and truly, towards Him Who created the heavens and the earth, and never shall I give partners to Allah. (Qur'an 6: 76–79)

Reading these verses may seem that Prophet Ibrahim (PBUH) initially took the stars, the moon and the sun as his Lord. However, these are rhetorical statements that he used to invite people towards the true God trough using logics. Like Prophet Ibrahim (PBUH), we all need to use our intellect to know Who our God is and the purpose He has assigned for us. Our purpose will be the Divine moral compass that will guide us through our life journey on earth. Prophet Ibrahim (PBUH) accepted his

Creator as his God and rejected everything else. Don't you find it logical? Find the truth and truth shall set you free. In the Qur'an, Allah asks the following question and want us to reflect on that.

> Were they created of nothing, or were they themselves the creators? (Qur'an 52: 35)

I hope you will agree that we do not do any significant activities without any purpose. For example, we buy a product either to use it ourselves or to present it to someone or to feel good by having it in our possession. Likewise, the supreme Creator Who is the Creator of the universe would not have created the most intelligent living creatures on earth without any purpose. Allah mentions in the Qur'an:

> Did you then think that We had created you in jest, and that you would not be brought back to Us (for account)? (Qur'an 23: 115)

This verse explicitly mentions that there is a purpose behind the creation of human beings, and they will be accountable for their deeds. This should sound logical and fare. Let us think about any job. Is there a job in the world where our employer will pay us but will not evaluate our performance?

As we will stand for a trial on the Day of Judgment, we need to have a clear perception of the purpose of life. Knowing the purpose of life will not just help us pursue success in eternal life, it will also help us find the meaning of our life in this world. In the Qur'an, Allah has mentioned that the only reason He has created human beings and jinn is to worship Him.

> And I (Allah) created not the jinns and humans except they should worship Me (Alone). (Qur'an 51: 56)

Therefore, the purpose of human beings is simple, and that is to worship their Creator (Allah). It is worth noticing the positioning of "NOT" in the above verse of the Qur'an. This has a significant bearing in deconstructing the meaning of this verse. This means the purpose of life is only to worship our Creator. Although worship involves formal and informal, obligatory and nonobligatory prayers, it is not limited to obligatory worships/ prayers such as Salah (Prayers), Siyam (Fasting), Zakah (Almsgiving) and Hajj (Pilgrimage). Leading our life following the guidelines prescribed by God is the real manifestation of worship. Our every act can be treated as worship so long it is done under the guidance of our Creator and following the way His messenger, Prophet Muhammad (PBUH). The aim of worship is to seek the pleasure of our Lord, Allah, through obeying His commandments. Allah wants us to work and live our livelihood correctly and honestly. He also wants us to sleep and take rest so that we can regain energy and be more productive. This is why the days and nights are created.

> And (have We not) created you in pairs, And made your sleep for rest, And made the night as a covering, And made

> the day as a means of subsistence? (Qur'an 78: 8-11)

Thus, Allah wants humankind to live a balanced life and guides them through the Divine words brought by the messengers: Qur'an is the final revelation for the human beings brought by the last messenger, Prophet Muhammad (PBUH). Everything we do can be considered as worship if it is done according to the teachings of Qur'an. Prophet Muhammad (PBUH) displayed the teachings of Qur'an for our reference. The essence of worship is manifested through complete faith and obedience to Allah. Worship encompasses every single activity of life as long as those are done for the sake of Allah. For example, the proper conduct of a person with his family members, neighbours, and community, in general, is an act of worship. Likewise, earning an honest livelihood and maintaining the family with honest earning is also worship. In a word, worship is the most essential part of human beings who are God's vicegerent on earth.

To summarise the purpose of life in simple words, let me conclude this chapter with a true story. In my quest to unveil the meaning of life, besides my secondary research, I had asked many people about their purpose of life formally and informally and found different answers. Some of these are: *to be happy in life; to live life on one's own terms; to achieve financial freedom; to achieve peace and tranquillity*; and many more. However, I was fascinated when I talked to one of my course-mates from

Bangladesh Navy, Afzal Hossain. His shortest answer simply amazed me. Both Afzal and I joined the Bangladesh Navy about thirty years before. We had our initial cadet training together in the Bangladesh Naval Academy and on-board Bangladesh Navy Frigates. Then with a scholarship, Afzal went to Germany and was commissioned in the German Navy. He is currently a Commodore in the Bangladesh Navy. However, when I asked him the question, he was a Captain, working as a Director at the Naval Headquarters. Afzal also attended his second staff college in the US Navy. He is one of the most talented officers in our batch and in the Navy. What Afzal mentioned were simply two words: grateful and useful. I found that these two words are very relevant in explaining the purpose of life.

To be Grateful

We need to be 'grateful' to our Lord through our submission to Him, for He has created the universe and us so that we can experience His blessings in every breath we take. Due to Covid-19, we could realise God's mercy and blessings upon us. We know how expensive the air ventilators are. Can you imagine how merciful is our Lord, Who is providing us with free oxygen 24 hours a day and seven days a week?

To be Useful

We also need to be 'useful' to all the creations of God, i.e., human beings and other creations through rendering our services to them. In that way, we can respond to our commitment to others. Life is not about earning money but to live happily. Research in psychology has revealed that true happiness comes at the service of others and pursuing meaning and fulfilment. In the Qur'an (49:13), Allah has mentioned that He has created human beings from a pair of parents and divided them into nations and tribes so that they can know each other. In other words, the diversity among human beings should not separate them, instead encourage them to stand for each other with a helping hand.

THE PERCEPTION AND REALITY OF SUCCESS

While discussing the purpose of life, it is essential to have an understanding of the real success of life as we are, by nature, inclined to success. Apparently, behind all the hard work we do in our lives is to become successful. However, real success may not be what we perceive to be a success. The Qur'an has explained the real success clearly. This has important implications in our life in setting priorities.

> Every soul shall have a taste of death: And only on the Day of Judgment shall you be paid your full recompense. Only he who is saved far from the fire and admitted to the garden will have

attained the object (of life): For the life of this world is but goods and chattels of deception. (Qur'an 3:185)

Let us now analyse this verse to deconstruct the meaning of real success.

> *"Every soul shall have a taste of death"* signifies that we are born to die, and there is no way to escape from death. As a leader, we need to think strategically with a long-term mind-set, considering life beyond our death. This worldly life is for a limited term and uncertain as we have no knowledge when death overtakes us. The eternal life is the only certainty, and as a leader, with strategic mind-set, we need to strive for that.

> *"And only on the Day of Judgment shall you be paid your full recompense"* signifies that we will be answerable for our deeds on the Day of Judgment and will be taken into account. Nothing will be out of records. This gives leaders a sense of accountability to the supreme Lord of this universe. This should encourage the leaders to take the righteous path to influence and serve their people rather than manipulate them.

> *"Only he who is saved far from the fire and admitted to the garden will have attained the object (of life)"* signifies that the real success is to save ourselves from the hellfire and be rewarded with paradise. This clause teaches the leaders and human beings the real criterion of success. Leaders are warned that their power and wealth will be of no use if they misuse them and end up in hell.

> *"For the life of this world is but goods and chattels of deception"* signifies that the life of this world is nothing but a play of deception, and we keep on running after

power, position, and wealth, but these have no real value towards our ultimate success. This is a warning for the leaders that they should not be deceived by the glitters of this world. This should help them prioritise between worldly and eternal life.

Therefore, this verse clearly explains that the real success of life is to save ourselves from the hellfire and entering into paradise in eternal life. In the previous chapter, we have revealed that life in this world is for a term and test as God's vicegerent. So, we need to design our lives in the submission of God and service to humanity. And, while doing so, we need to follow the commands of our Lord. In the Qur'an (23:1-11), Allah has also unveiled the qualities of the ultimate winners who will enter into paradise.

1. The believers must (eventually) win through –
2. Those who humble themselves in their prayers;
3. Who avoid vain talk;
4. Who are active in deeds of charity;
5. Who abstain from sex,
6. Except with those joined to them in the marriage bond, or (the captives) whom their right hands possess- for (in their case) they are free from blame,
7. But those whose desires exceed those limits are transgressors-
8. Those who faithfully observe their trusts and their covenants;
9. And who (strictly) guard their prayers –
10. These will be the heirs,
11. Who will inherit paradise: they will dwell in it (forever).

Thus, to be successful leaders should work to acquiring the qualities of believers and help their people to develop the same attributes. Many other verses unveil the further attributes of the believers who will be the winner in the eternal life.

> For, believers are those who, when Allah is mentioned, feel a tremor in their hearts, and when they hear His signs rehearsed, find their faith strengthened, and put (all) their trust in their Lord; Who establish regular prayers and spend (freely) out of the gifts We have given them for sustenance: Such in truth are the believers: they have grades of dignity with their Lord, and forgiveness, and generous sustenance. (Quran 8: 2 - 4)

As mentioned in the above verse, being fearful of their Lord differentiates the believers. Hearts of believing people shiver in fear whenever they hear the name of their Creator (Allah) and the verses of the Qur'an. The believers rely upon their Lord, and their rewards are reserved for eternal life. They are also granted the forgiveness of their Lord and enjoy noble provision as blessings of their Lord.

LEADERSHIP IMPLICATION

The clarity of the purpose of life and understanding of the real success criteria help leaders to set their moral gyro, enabling them to steer the right path. It will also help them empower their people to seek the right way. Thus, together they and their team can be successful both here and hereafter. The chapter teaches us that power, position and wealth have no value in the day of judgment if not used for the cause of Allah. The real success will be determined after our death, for which we need to live our lives with good deeds:

> "...He Who created death and life, that He may try which of you is best in deed: and He is the Exalted in Might, Oft-Forgiving; (Qur'an 67: 1-2)

Time is running out! We do not know the time when we will have to leave this world! To be successful, we need to have faith, do righteous deeds, and spread truth, and be patient as Allah says in the Qur'an (103: 1-3).

1. By (the token of) time (through the ages),
2. Verily man is in loss,
3. Except such as have faith, and do righteous deeds, and (join together) in the mutual teaching of truth, and of patience and constancy.

PART II

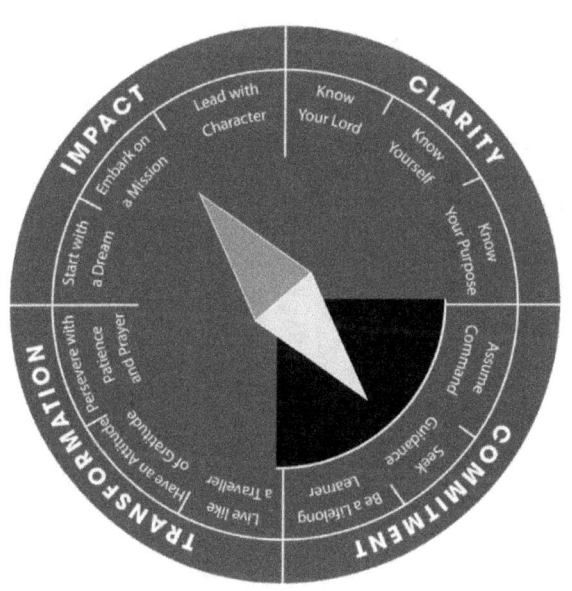

COMMITMENT

Although every ship has only one Commanding Officer, while working on-board naval ships, I learned that we are all indeed the Captains of our own lives and our successes follow when we assume command – in other words, take the responsibilities for our lives and make decisions.

The Author

4

ASSUME COMMAND
Take the Helm of Your Life

January 1st, 1990. One of my brothers, a Captain in the Bangladesh Army, dropped me at the Naval Academy, based in Chittagong, Bangladesh. My Cadet training started with a dream to be a commissioned officer in the Navy. When the tough training struck me from all sides, I was initially nervous, but soon I learned how to cope with any adverse situations. There are many memories, which I love to cherish from time to time. Time flew so fast that I often could not keep track of it. Then, one beautiful morning, I found myself on-board a Frigate doing my midshipman training. The life on-board warship was quite different from life onshore – mainly, the space is quite limited for many people to live in. It taught me how little we need in life and how vital the relationship is that we maintain with the fellow members of the team. I discovered that I could be entirely happy only with a bunk bed on-board the warship for me to sleep and a kit bag for me to carry my things when I am posted to another warship. When I saw myself amid the sea, I realised how little and insignificant I was in relation to this vast universe. In fact, the sailors' life is defined by their life on-board *ships* at *sea*, which is quite unique and can teach us many lessons that are invaluable for understanding the essence of leadership. As I reflect on my career in the Navy, I find that together ships and the sea make an excellent school for leadership and life.

One of the most important things that I learned on-board a warship during my service in the Navy was assuming the *Command of the Ship* by the Captain. In the Navy, there is a saying: m*y ship, my command.* 'Command' is a term used in the Navy, but, in my opinion, this is misunderstood most of the time. People often relate it to authority, power, and prestige, although in reality, it is not the case. Good leaders see it as an opportunity to serve others.

Through command, leaders in the Navy are given permission to serve their people instead of authority acquired to be served. 'Command' also means creating a culture and an environment where people will learn and grow to their full potential. However, based on my experience of serving in the Navy for over fifteen years and also experiencing life beyond the Navy, I believe that command has a profound significance in our lives, which can enable us to develop as leaders.

Although every ship has only one Commanding Officer, I learned that we are all indeed the Captains of our own lives, and our successes follow when we assume command - in other words, take the responsibilities for our lives and make decisions. God has empowered us with intellect and free will to be the architects of our own lives. The sooner we realise this reality, the sooner we can embark on a transformational journey to be successful not only in this life but also in the life hereafter.

The psychology of success suggests that it is not the circumstance, but our response to it that determines our success. To explain this point to my students, I often write an equation, $E + R = R$, on the whiteboard; and ask them a question: What condition makes this equation correct? They usually take 30 seconds to answer it, and in most of the cases, they say when E is equal to zero, which is correct answer. Then I rewrite the equation, "Event + Response = Result", and the students usually get the message. According to Brian Tracy, one of the world's top motivational public speakers, and a self-development author and coach, successful people do not complain about their circumstances; instead, they focus on their response. Thus, their response shapes their result (reality), i.e., their success. Instead of holding onto the current reality (circumstances), they create their new reality (result/ future).

While focusing on the *glorious future*, they make the best use of their *valuable present,* having no time to hold onto their *past*. If they had a dark *past,* they take lessons from it and enjoy the joy of navigating through the rough sea of life to find a safe harbour. When it comes to learning and growing, we are probably living in the best time in history. Learning and growing were never so much easier before. We have access to the vast amount of knowledge through online and offline; we can follow the leaders who inspire us through social media; we can take a high-quality online degree at a reasonable price. There was a time when companies used to take a few days to respond to customers' queries. People nowadays get a response to their questions from the president of a country through tweets in a few minutes. There is no reason to complain that you cannot learn and grow to be a leader. Leaders live like Captains - they not only take responsibility for their decisions and for their lives but also for their people. Since I left the Navy, I initially thought I will never experience this concept of 'assuming the command of the ship', but my perception changed when I joined a university in London as an academic.

While working as Associate Head of Research and Scholarship, I came across Dr Socrates Karidis, who joined the university to lead the Department of Accounting, Finance and Economics. During his first week, Socrates found me to discuss how research activities can be promoted further. I was pleasantly surprised by his initiative as he was not responsible for research. Unlike many other people who remain busy thinking about how they could be confirmed in their current roles, Socrates started to take the initiative in almost everything. Due to his prolong experience in research and scholarship, soon he became my boss, and I started following his strategic guidance. I started feeling proud to say to everyone that I report to Socrates, for the purpose of research and scholarship, which is no doubt an aspired area for many academics. A feeling started to run through me as if I am the Greek Philosopher Plato reporting to Socrates.

Interestingly, I found that Socrates is a Greek, having four academic degrees in economics, including a doctorate from a US university. This was the time my elder son got an admission into the London School of Economics and Political Science with a full scholarship to study economics and government. Seeing my son's workloads, I could sense how difficult it is to complete even one degree in economics, let alone four degrees. This was another reason Socrates easily influenced me by his expert power. It may be mentioned that to influence their people, leaders often use fives types of power: coercive power, expert power, legitimate power, referent power, and reward power where expert power is categorised as a personal power which leaders achieve due to their knowledge and expertise (Northouse, 2013). Power literature is also inextricably linked with leadership literature and whether we like it or not, conceptualising leadership is not complete without understanding various powers. Even though we were not ancient Greek philosophers, I wanted to develop similar relationships with Socrates that Plato had with his teacher.

While working with Socrates, at times, I also felt that I was reporting to *Little John*. Socrates, with a height of six feet six inches, looked like Little John, a member of Robin Hood's team. Robin Hood is a legendary heroic pirate, featured in English folklore, literature, and film; and *Little John* was his primary companion. I was a fan of Robin Hood and Little John since I read about them during my childhood. This may be a reason for me to choose the University of Nottingham for my PhD, and enjoy the city of Robin Hood. However, with his PhD from a US university and research experience in economics, Socrates was far more qualified and intelligent than both Little John and Robin Hood. His expert power kept on surprising me with some charismatic outputs.

While I had been waiting for six months to get the research policy approved, he got it approved in less than a month. For this, he had to convince the academic and executive boards of the university, and I am sure it was his knowledge and not his 6 feet 6 inches height that influenced the members of the board to sign this off. The pleasant surprise came when he was hired as the Associate Pro-Vice-Chancellor in a few months. Socrates reminded me about a leadership principle, assuming the command of the ship, which I learned in the Navy. As Associate Pro-Vice-Chancellor, Socrates assumed the command with absolute responsibility, demanding academics to claim and reclaim their identity. We all could feel the energy going through the university as Socrates took over this senior leadership role. In his words, the two core areas that shape an academic's identity are research and teaching. Although Socrates is an experienced researcher who writes his paper during the weekends (he shared his experience of writing paper with me), he created a 'work plan' that had an excellent provision to support the research initiatives within the university. The day he was explaining the plan in front of the academics, one thing caught my attention. He said with a calm and confident voice:

> "If we plan a new academic's time with eighty per cent of teaching and twenty per cent of admin works, we are indeed planning to destroy his career".

He further said: "The academics who have already developed their career as a researcher with good publication records should help to free up some time for the new academics, allowing them to build up their research portfolio". This shows his sincerity in creating an environment to support the academics in research besides their teaching commitments. This is what 'command' means in the Navy: to create an environment where people can learn, grow, deliver their best, and thrive.

Another thing that caught my attention about Socrates's leadership trait was his accessibility to people. He likes to be a man of happening by being present everywhere. I believe he can work without an intercom as he prefers to come and talk to people in person, which makes a huge difference when it comes to creating a people-centric culture. Besides, it is reasonably easy to meet him anytime unless he is in the middle of a crucial assignment. He has a round table in his room, and when talking to people, he always sits across this table. I have seen many leaders having an extra table in their room, which they use for the meeting. However, a round table has an advantage due to its shape. None can take advantage of *positional authority* that comes with where someone sits across the table. There is research that identified exciting facts about the shape of the table and the quality of discussions it facilitates.

> "To their surprise, none of those things seemed to matter much. What did matter, it turned out, was the shape of the table in the jury room! In courtrooms where there is was a rectangular table, the junior sitting at the head of the table (even if that person wasn't the jury foreman) tended to dominate the conversation. This kept some juniors from sharing their points of view as openly. But in jury rooms

that had a round or oval table, the juniors tended to be more egalitarian and their debate of the facts was more through and robust. The team concluded it was those juries with round tables that came to the most accurate and just verdicts." (Smith, 2012, p. 1-2)

When we usually have meetings sitting around a rectangular table, I never saw Socrates seated in the corner unless that is the seat left, even if he was the Chair of the meeting. Thus, it sends a message that everyone is equally important, and their opinions count. However, when time demands a bit of direction, he does not hesitate to influence the conversation. I found Socrates had a leadership style that I have seen in the Navy.

People often think that military leaderships are authoritarian. That is just a perception and not always correct. The modern-day military leaders practice egalitarian leadership approach to build a dynamic organisation. Recently, I had an opportunity to interview two professionally well-known senior officers in the Bangladesh Navy, one of whom is currently at the helm of the service and a four-star Admiral. I was pleasantly surprised to see his humility when he agreed to talk to me at short notice. When I wanted to know about his leadership style, he mentioned about the egalitarian approach. He said that the most substantial part of his leadership style is his accessibility to his people. He precisely mentioned that people are not at all frightened to meet him and talk to him. This is quite unusual for a four-star Admiral, and initially, I was trying to figure out how it helps a leader. Then he explained it to me:

> "You know, the success of a leader depends to a great extent upon the quality of his decisions, and often the quality of decisions depends upon the quality of information leaders are exposed to. When leaders can create a system that provides a smooth flow of information, they are empowered to make better decisions. If your people are afraid of you, you are unlikely to get the right information. They will tell what pleases you and not what the reality is."

The words of the four-star Admiral, sitting at the helm of a three-dimensional Navy with the surface, air and underwater capabilities amazed me. His words tell a lot about his relationship with people and his preference for egalitarian leadership over authoritarian leadership. Furthermore, he mentioned his passion for knowledge and his interest to take every opportunity to train people no matter whatever their ranks are. You might be expecting a four-star Admiral will take all chances to shine by talking about all the big things he has accomplished while training in home and abroad and working as part of the senior strategic team of the country. On the contrary, he cited examples where he had trained people at the very root-level in the course of his work. I was astonished to hear about the case of one junior non-continuous service sailor with whom he consulted about the provisions of some skill-development training that can help them in finding jobs once they retire. He had this conversation when he was a two-star Admiral and Assistant Chief of Naval Staff.

Another example was an incident where another junior sailor working in his official residence committed a mistake despite him explaining the task very clearly as the Chief of the Naval Staff, but he only responded by allowing him the time for reflection. The sailor then took the further initiative and accomplished the job in a few hours, demonstrating nothing but excellence. While saying this, he clarified his position very frankly and mentioned that he is ready to tolerate mistakes but not the decay in honesty. He went on saying:

> "As a human being, every one of us has self-respect and dignity, and our honesty preserves our dignity. When we understand this, we can be more careful about upholding our honesty."

This reminds me about one invaluable leadership trait I learned while serving in the Navy that helps leaders to earn the trust of the people they are entrusted to serve. It is 'integrity'. I first learnt about integrity while working on-board the warships. To remain floated a ship has to maintain watertight integrity. There should not be any hole on the hull of the ship that remains underwater. Even a small hole, if not appropriately managed, can sink the ship through flooding. The same is the case for a leader who needs integrity more than anything. By integrity, I do not mean honesty rather uncompromising honesty. True leaders should not compromise with honesty and never sell their character under any situation. Integrity is a trait that defines the character of the leader. Clark (2016) has developed a model with two fundamental dimensions of leadership: *character* and *competence*. Through this model, he identified four types of leaders:

Leaders with high character and high competence are great leaders. They take the organisations forward and develop more great leaders. Leaders with low characters and low competence are failed leaders. They are not definitely suitable for organisations, and in most cases are fired. Leaders with high character and low competence are ineffective leaders. However, if they are surrounded by other competent leaders and managers, they can take the organisation forward, and through training, they also overcome their limitations. Leaders with low character and high competence are dangerous leaders. Usually, people cannot catch their dishonesty, and they get plenty of opportunities to server their personal interest and destroy the organisations and in many cases their subordinates character as well. The lessons that I have learned in the Navy have shaped my leadership thinking, and I have just shared a few as this book is not about naval leadership. While I miss my days in the Navy, these are the lessons that keep me going. Indeed, I realised the value of my naval experiences more intensely after I had voluntarily left the Navy and whenever I cherished my sweet memories. Often I feel my heart is still in the Navy. Tracey (2014, p.95) identified integrity as "The Essential Quality of Leadership". Drawing on personal life experience, he mentioned the following that explains the crucks of leadership to a great extent in just a few lines:

> "IN AN EXECUTIVE boardroom, I once heard one of the richest men in America make a statement that I never forgot. "It seems to me" he said, "that integrity isn't really a value in itself; it is simply the value that guarantees all the other values." Whenever I hold a strategic planning session, the first value that all the executives agree on is integrity. Leaders know that integrity, trust, and credibility are foundations of leadership." (Tracey, 2014, p.95)

Let's come back to my conversation with the Admiral again. As I worked in the same Navy before my voluntary retirement fifteen years before, I used to know him although I never had the opportunity to serve under his command. However, I was always keen to work for him because of the professional reputation that he had developed. Although he is now a four-star Admiral, his path to this position was not at all rosy, and there are many officers, who would argue that he should have been on the helm long before. I was inquisitive to know about the not-so-rosy time of his career and how he maintained his enthusiasm during those difficult times. My objective was nothing but to get some wisdom for my readers as every one of us face a challenging time in our career. In response to my question, he mentioned that he had never wanted to stand against the course that nature has set in his life. He believes what comes naturally is always good for us, and our job is to do what we can to the best possible way. I was further, impressed by his simplicity while answering my question: what legacy would you like to leave behind? He paused a little and said:

> "Well, I have never thought about leaving a legacy. I was more concerned to accomplish the job I was entrusted with to the best possible way so that the organisation is benefitted."

I understood one of the strengths of his leadership is his simplicity and his personal accountability to the job he is entrusted to accomplish – his accountability to himself and to his people. This brings me to the end of this chapter by bringing the concept of assuming the command once again. In fact, the journey to leadership starts with taking complete responsibility by assuming the command of your ship called life. If you do not take responsibility for your life and do whatever it takes you to be successful as a person and as a leader, no one else can help you. If you want to be knowledgeable, you need to read, observe, learn and reflect. If you're going to increase your adaptability, you need to transform yourself while going through struggles and overcoming adversities. If you want to be trusted as a leader, you need to develop your character and value proposition. If you want to create a legacy, you need to make an impact in the world. In the end, you are the Captain of your life, but your success depends on whether you assume the command or not. The dimensions of assuming the command means: Taking responsibility, making decision, taking action, reflect and learn from mistake to better start the cycle again. Do not forget that command is an opportunity that comes in the form of trust to serve your people and create an environment where they flourish. How your people grow determines how good your command is. Your people are the mirror of your command.

Allah is the light of the heavens and the earth. The example of His light is like a niche within which is a lamp, the lamp is within glass, the glass as if it were a pearly [white] star lit from [the oil of] a blessed olive tree, neither of the east nor of the west, whose oil would almost glow even if untouched by fire. Light upon light. Allah guides to His light whom He wills. And Allah presents examples for the people, and Allah is knowing of all things.

(Qur'an 24:35)

5

SEEK GUIDANCE
Find Freedom through Faith

In Part I: *Clarity*, we have addressed three crucial questions: Who is your Creator? Who are you? What is your purpose in life? Then in Chapter 6, we have discussed the importance of assuming the command of your life. What is next? While we need to get ourselves seated in the captain's chair and take responsibility for our lives, we also need to continue seeking the guidance of our Creator as we are His lieutenants on earth with a grand purpose. In the Qur'an (5: 15–16), Allah mentions the following:

> O people of the Book! There has come to you our messenger, revealing to you much that you used to hide in the Book, and passing over much (that is now

> unnecessary): There has come to you from Allah a (new) light and a perspicuous book, -
>
> With which Allah guides all who seek His good pleasure to ways of peace and safety, and leads them out of darkness, by His Will, unto the light, - guides them to a path that is straight.

Seeking guidance is about finding the right direction towards which you can lead your life during your short stay on earth – may be sixty, seventy, eighty or even hundred years. That is too short in comparison to the infinite life hereafter. Now the question is how we can find the right direction. Well, God has sent messengers to guide humankind so that they understand what is right and what is wrong and how to qualify in the test of life on earth.

> Who receive guidance, receive it for his own benefit: who goes astray does so to his own loss: No bearer of burdens can bear the burden of another: nor would We visit with Our wrath until We had sent an apostle (to give warning). (Qur'an 17:15)

As mentioned in the above verse, God has sent His Messengers over the ages to guide the human beings, and the last and final messenger is Prophet Muhammad (PBUH), who brought the final revelation of God for humankind: The Holy Qur'an. Therefore, the Qur'an and the life of the Prophet are the real guidance for human beings. As we follow the manufacturer's manual while using a complex product, we need to follow the direction of our Creator to operate our lives rightly.

THE ART OF SEEKING GUIDANCE

While taking the Qur'an as the source of guidance sent by our Creator, let us carefully read the first Surah Al-Fatihah. Indeed, the first Surah of the Qur'an (1: 1-7) is a prayer to seek guidance from our Lord.

1. In the name of Allah, Most Gracious, Most Merciful.
2. Praise be to Allah, the Cherisher and Sustainer of the worlds;
3. Most Gracious, Most Merciful;
4. Master of the Day of Judgment.
5. You do we worship, and Your aid we seek.
6. Show us the straight way,
7. The way of those on whom You have bestowed Your Grace, those whose (portion) is not wrath, and who go not astray.

If you carefully ponder on the meaning of the Surah, you will also notice a structure of seeking the guidance of our Lord. You will see that the Surah starts with the praise of our Lord (verse 1-3) and ends with seeking His guidance (verse 6 -7). The middle of the Surah introduces our Lord as the Master of the Day of Judgment (verse 4) whom we worship only and ask for help (verse 5). Therefore, the middle of the Surah establishes Lord-slave relationship between our Creator and us. Please note, understanding of the message of this holy book, which is God's words, is part of seeking guidance. We can also see that this Surah is placed strategically - at the very beginning of the Qur'an – so that the readers can proceed with a desire to seek guidance from the Lord of the universe. From this Surah, we can deduce a 4-step process for seeking guidance.

> *1. Praise and Thank:* Praise and thank your Lord using His beautiful names and attributes.
>
> *2. Feeling Master-Slave Relationship:* Conceptualise and acknowledge His status, power and dominion. We need to have a deep sense of feeling and a firm conviction in our heart that we are the subjects, and He is our Master.
>
> *3. Freedom though Submission:* Worship is reserved for our Lord only, and He is the Only One to seek help from. This will free us from all sorts of slavery.
>
> *4. Seek Guidance:* Finally, we need to ask for guidance from our Lord so that we can be shown the right path, taken by those who have been successful.

There is also a profound message in this Surah: the best thing human beings can ask from their Lord is guidance. As the whole Qur'an encompasses advices for human beings (the codes of leading our life), Surah Al-Fatihah prepares the readers with a mindset to understand the message, finding guidance as they make their journey through the Divine revelation.

As you progress to the next Surah, you will notice a clear statement in verse number 2 that I am sure you have never come across in any other book. This verse has made many people ponder, and eventually, through their further research, they agreed that Qur'an is the words of God. Following are five verse of the Qur'an (2:1-5)

1. Alif Lam Mim
2. This is the book; in it is guidance sure, without doubt, to those who fear Allah.
3. Who believe in the unseen, are steadfast in prayer, and spend out of what We have provided for them;
4. And who believe in the revelation sent to you, and sent before your time, and (in their hearts) have the assurance of the hereafter.
5. They are on (true) guidance, from their Lord, and it is these who will prosper.

So, what do you find here? Allah is making a clear statement that there is no doubt in the Qur'an. How can there be any doubt when it has come from the Creator of the universe? Allah gives us a warning that to seek the guidance of our Lord, we need to pass the test of faith using our intellect. Drawing on the essence of these verses following the Tafsir of Ibnu Katsir, we can deduce that this book will only be a source of guidance for those who meet the following criteria:

1. Be conscious of God;
2. Believe in the unseen;
3. Establish prayer;
4. Give obligatory charity;
5. Believe in the Qur'an, which has been revealed to Prophet Muhammad (PBUH);
6. Believe in what was revealed to other messengers of God before; and
7. Believe in the life hereafter with certainty

The verse, "…and (in their hearts) have the assurance of the hereafter" (Qur'an 2:4) gives individuals (who gets guidance) a strategic orientation, i.e. the long-term orientation which allow them to ponder on their life beyond death. Another critical criterion mentioned in other verses of the Qur'an to get guidance is to be fearful of our Lord.

> O you who have believed, if you fear God, He will grant you a criterion and will remove from you your misdeeds and forgive you. And God is the possessor of great bounty. (Qur'an 8: 29)
>
> O you who have believed, fear God as He should be feared and do not die except as Muslims [in submission to Him] (Qur'an 3: 102)

Individuals are unlikely to pay heed to the message of God unless His punishment in the hereafter creates fear in their heart. In the Qur'an, God has used mercy and punishment to create hope and fear, respectively, in the hearts of His subjects. However, forgiveness (mercy) comes twice the times than sentence (punishment), pointing the kindness of our Lord. Punishment can also be viewed as compassion when it is used to guide people so that they can come back to the right path. In fact, the most precious gift an individual can have is the guidance of their Lord so that they can be successful in the never-ending eternal life. Think for a moment. If you have the guidance of your Lord, do you need anything else? If you are confused and cannot answer this question with certainty, let me ask you another question. What if you have started a business and Bill Gates, Warren Buffett and Jeff Bezos come to guide you in managing it? Don't you have the best support? Certainly, yes. They are the three of the most successful businesspersons in the world, and their organisations have made a significant impact in the world. Likewise, when we have the guidance of the Lord of the universe, what else do we need? In regards to guidance, another verse of the Qur'an (known as Ayat-un-Nur, i.e. The Verse of Light) is remarkably significant. In this verse, Allah introduces Him as the lights of the heavens and the earth.

> Allah is the light of the heavens and the earth. The example of His light is like a niche within which is a lamp, the lamp is within glass, the glass as if it were a pearly [white] star lit from [the oil of] a blessed olive tree, neither of the east nor of the west, whose oil would almost glow even if untouched by fire. Light upon light. Allah guides to His light whom He wills. And Allah presents examples for the people, and Allah is knowing of all things. (Qur'an 24:35)

To comprehend the essence of this verse, besides my ordinary explanation, I welcome you to consult the opinions of the prominent scholars of the Qur'an. Allah has used several beautiful and thought-provoking parables in this verse to let humankind ponder and understand the essence of His message. This verse is one of the best parables used in the Qur'an for its metaphorical meaning, carrying a central message regarding guidance. The metaphorical eloquence of this verse – where there are parables within the parable – will amaze you, I believe. First, it starts with a parable of 'light': "Allah is the lights of the heavens and the earth". Let us pause and think for a moment. What is the purpose of light? What if there is no light? The answer is simple. In the presence of light, we can see; in the absence of it, we cannot see even we have perfect eyesight. Likewise, in the absence of the light of Allah (Who is the only provider of guidance), we cannot contemplate the 'reality' of life. The parable - "Allah is the lights of heavens and earth" - also means that everything in heaven and earth needs the lights (i.e. the guidance) of Allah (Khan, 2013). The other parables are as follows:

1. Niche (within which there is a lamp),
2. Lamp (placed within the glass),
3. Glass (like a star),
4. Oil (of a blessed olive tree), lighting the lamp
5. The olive tree (neither from the east nor from the west)
6. The oil glow without being touched by fire

Drawing on Khan (2013), these parables can be explained as follows:

1. The niche can be compared with our rib case – the room we have insight our chest;
2. There is glass around the niche – the purpose the glass is to spread the light;
3. The lamp inside the niche can be compared with our heart;
4. The olive tree can be compared with the ribs of our chest that surround our heart;
5. Oil can be compared with the message of Allah.
6. The Qur'an is the source of guidance.

Therefore, the last parable – 'light upon light' – means when the light of Allah's revelation falls upon our heart, do we get guidance. Now, the question is who gets this guidance. The answer is in the same verse: (a) the one Allah wills and (b) the one who makes a sincere endeavour and seek the guidance of his Creator. Thus, we need to sincerely seek the guidance of our Lord. And Allah guides the believers with his light, further mentioned in Surah Baqarah of the Qur'an.

> Allah is the Protector of those who have faith: from the depths of darkness He will lead them forth into light. Of those who reject faith the patrons are the evil ones: from light they will lead them forth into the depths of darkness. They will be companions of the fire, to dwell therein (forever). (Qur'an 2: 257).

Thus, in the Qur'an, clearly, there is guidance for the believers. It can get them out of darkness into the light. Furthermore, the following verses from *Surah Ibrahim (Qur'an 14:1-4)* convey profound lessons to individuals to *view life from a long-term perspective*. Here, long-term is not defined as over five or ten years but the eternal life after death.

1. Alif, Lam, Ra. A book which We have revealed unto you, in order that you might lead mankind out of the depths of darkness into light - by the leave of their Lord - to the Way of (Him) the Exalted in power, worthy of all Praise!-
2. Of Allah, to Whom do belong all things in the heavens and on earth! But alas for the unbelievers a terrible penalty (their unfaith will bring them)!-

3. Those who love the life of this world more than the hereafter, who hinder (men) from the path of Allah and seek therein something crooked: they are astray by a long distance.
4. We sent not an apostle except (to teach) in the language of his (own) people, in order to make (things) clear to them. Now Allah leaves straying those whom He pleases and guides whom He pleases: and He is Exalted in power, full of Wisdom.

The wide range of leadership and strategy literature suggests that strategy is about making the right choice amongst various options, and great leaders know their priorities. In these verses, God is urging people to use strategic lens while conceptualising life. These verses call believers with a strategic direction, enabling them to prioritise the infinite life hereafter over the short life on earth. On the other hand, some people are short-term oriented. To them, their life on earth is far more lucrative than the eternal life after death. In fact, some people even do not believe in the hereafter. For them, I recommend my book, The Purpose of Life: Understanding the Divine Message through the Lens of Leadership and Strategy. I believe, the last part of the book, To Believe or Not to Believe, will give you enough to think.

CASE STUDIES

What would you do if you were inside the shoes of Shahin Ahsan? Shahin was my coursemate in Bangladesh Navy.

Like me, Shahin also voluntarily retired with a dream to leverage his knowledge, skills and experience in the corporate world. With an engineering degree from the Bangladesh University of Engineering and Technology and over ten years of experience in the Navy, his eyes were on Silicon Valley. While preparing as an operational engineer in the Navy, he occasionally dreamed of working there. After his retirement, he went to the USA to pursue this dream. Taking a master degree in Electrical and Electronics Engineering turned out to be an effective strategy. He started the journey leaving his family back home. With minimal fund at hand, life tested him harder. He could run himself for two months at best and needed a part-time job. One of his friends managed him a job, which would give him enough money to complete his study. On the first day at work, he discovered that he has to sell alcohol as part of the job. He was in a critical situation. He needed a job to bear all his costs, but the Qur'an, which he considers to be his moral compass, does not allow him to deal with (buy/sell) alcohol. He was in a dilemma. He thought very strategically: 'short-term' vs 'long-term'. His definition of 'short-term' was this life while the 'long-term' was eternal life. Shahin refused to take the job, leaving him on an uncertain future. But he kept on applying with a faith in God that he would be able to find something. Finally, he got a call from a Professor of his department who is well-connected with the industry. Shahin was hired as a research assistant to support the Professor on his new research project. This gave him enough money to complete his masters and bring his family to the USA. The opportunity to work on this project gave him exposure to the corporate world. Later, Shahin did not face further problems. He was hired as an Engineer in a semiconductor company soon after finishing his final exam. He is ever grateful to his Lord. Shahin is now a *Principal Engineer*, working at the R&D department of a technology company with its Headquarter in Silicon Valley. He is part of several projects that are making a positive impact on a global scale. What would you do if you had been in the shoes of Shahin Ahsan? Allah tests people, but those who patiently persevere are the winners at the end. Whenever I talked to Shahin, he always told me that he could feel the blessings of God, in every stage of his life. We all can experience the mercy of God. We just need to patiently persevere.

LEADERSHIP IMPLICATION

Faith in God has a significant implication on our life and the way we lead as a leader. Faith in God - who is (a) the Creator of the whole universe and every created thing in it including the humankind, (b) the source of all power, and (c) the owner of the Day of Judgment - gives us the real freedom through establishing a Master-slave relationship. By believing (with its all facets) in God, and acknowledging that He is the only one worthy of our worships, we can free ourselves from the direct or indirect slavery of any other person and things such as wealth, fame, titles, luxuries, and so on. Faith in God makes the leaders and the humankind accountable to God, saving them from uncontrolled behaviour as they will have to answer for their deeds on the Day of Judgment.

> On that day will men proceed in companies sorted out, to be shown the deeds that they (had done). Then shall anyone who has done an atom's weight of good, see it! And anyone who has done an atom's weight of evil, shall see it. (Qur'an 99: 6-8)

Faith in God also helps the leaders in going through the worldly challenges easily, knowing that life on earth is a test and challenges are part of life – even an opportunity (often reminders) to come back to the path of Allah. Qur'an (2:155-156) says:

> Be sure we shall test you with something of fear and hunger, some loss in goods or lives or the fruits (of your toil), but give glad tidings to those who patiently persevere,
>
> Who say, when afflicted with calamity: "To Allah we belong, and to Him is our return"-

Finally, faith in God, helps the leaders to take the risk when needed, as a leader who has complete faith in God knows that the only certainty is God (Qur'an 2:255 and 112:1-4). Faith in God also teaches us to think strategically: the next life is infinite and this life is a test.

Read: In the Name of your Lord who created.
Created man from a clot.
Read: And your Lord is the Most Generous.
He who taught by the pen.
Taught man what he never knew.

(Qur'an 96: 1-5)

6

BE A LIFELONG LEARNER
Develop the Third Eye

During the "Cadet Sea Training", my first experience of working on-board worship started as a "Cadet Lookout". As I reported to the Officer of the Watch (OOW) on the Frigate, he positioned me on the bridge wing and handed me over a binocular. My job was to look through the sea surface and above, as much as I can see. I was looking for any ships or boats on a probable collision course, and fishing nets or any objects that could be dangerous for our ship. In a bright sunny day when the visibility is excellent, I could see only up to the horizon. We all have two eyes, and we can see up to the horizon in ideal condition.

What is our horizon, and how can we extend it so that we can see farther? Working as a "Ship's Lookout", I found that although an excellent binocular had widened my horizon I was missing many objects that were within my eyesight. I could not figure out how the Midshipman standing inside the bridge could see things that I could not from the bridge wing, and how the OOW could see what the Midshipman could not.

When I became a Midshipman and later started working as OOW, things became clear to me. Insight that comes with knowledge and experience, gives us a better sight. We all have two eyes, and if we want to see things with our eyes, we can only see so far and so much. The vision of our eyes has a limitation. The real leaders have a third eye: The gut, the intuition. This third eye enables the leaders to see beyond the horizon (future) no matter how poor (uncertain) the visibility is.

The third eye envisions us to see things with certainty. In the Qur'an (102:1-8), Allah has used two beautiful metaphors to explain the certainty that comes from our vision and knowledge: *(1) Ilm-ul-yaqeen* (the knowledge of certainty) and *(2) Ayn-ul-yaqeen* (the vision of certainty).

1. The mutual rivalry for piling up (the good things of this world) diverts you (from the more serious things),
2. Until you visit the graves.
3. But nay, you soon shall know (the reality).
4. Again, you soon shall know!

5. Nay, were you to know with certainty of mind, (you would beware!)
6. You shall certainly see hellfire!
7. Again, you shall see it with certainty of sight!
8. Then, shall you be questioned that day about the joy (you indulged in!).

In this Surah, Allah clearly mentions that people are on a dangerous course competing for wealth with each other and missing the most significant things in life. To understand what matters, they use the vision of certainty (Ayn-ul-yaqeen). This strategy of seeing things will not save them in eternal life as their strategic choices in this life will be focused on the wrong things. On the other hand, knowledge of certainty (Ilm-ul-yaqeen) can empower them to make the right strategic choices here, leading to success in the hereafter. In fact, it is the power of knowledge that put into practice becomes wisdom, giving leaders the third eye and enabling them to see through the future. Knowledge[2] empowers us to know the truth. Truth can set us free, bringing us from the darkness of ignorance into the lights of reality. However, knowledge is power when it is correct, and we can use it to differentiate what is right from what is wrong. To be beneficial, the credibility of sources and appropriate applications of knowledge are necessary. The incorrect knowledge, coming from unreliable sources, can have a detrimental effect on our lives. In the Qur'an, Allah

---

[2] By knowledge, we refer to correct knowledge, which, according to the Oxford dictionary, refers to as "the information, understanding and skills that you gain through education or experience."

mentions that those who have knowledge are different from those who don't.

> Is one who is devoutly obedient during periods of the night, prostrating and standing [in prayer], fearing the hereafter and hoping for the mercy of his Lord, [like one who does not]? Say, "Are those who know equal to those who do not know?" Only they will remember [who are] people of understanding. (Qur'an 39:9)

THE IMPORTANCE OF KNOWLEDGE

Knowledge has a very high status in Islam. Knowledge helps people to know their Creator. Thinking, reasoning, and understanding are also linked to knowledge in different ways. Knowledge can help us use our reasoning and deepen our understanding. Again, using reasoning, we can increase our knowledge and understanding of our Creator. Thus, people who like to think and use reasons (Ulul Albab[3]) have a special position to Allah.

> Behold! in the creation of the heavens and the earth; in the alternation of the night and the day; in the sailing of the ships through the ocean for the profit of mankind; in the rain which Allah sends down from the skies, and the life which He gives therewith to an earth that is dead; in the beasts of all kinds that He scatters through the earth; in the change of the winds, and the clouds which they trail like their slaves between the sky and the earth;- (Here) indeed

---

[3] Ulul Albab is an Arabic word used in the Qur'an, which means people of intellect or people of understanding.

are signs for a people that are wise. (Qur'an 2: 164)

A journey in seeking knowledge has the potential to increase our power of reasoning and empower us to understand the greatness of our Creator through the cosmological signs of His creations all around us. The people of knowledge have been given a special honour to testify the oneness of God along with God Himself and the angels as mentioned in the following verse.

> There is no god but He: That is the witness of Allah, His angels, and those endued with knowledge, standing firm on justice. There is no god but He, the exalted in power, the wise. (Qur'an 3:18)

One of the greatest supplications mentioned in the Qur'an teaches us that the best thing humankind should seek from their Lord is knowledge – not wealth, fame, and power because the application of knowledge can give us all those.

> High above all is Allah, the King, the Truth! Be not in haste with the Qur'an before its revelation to you is completed, but say, "O my Lord! advance me in knowledge. (Qur'an 20: 114)

Thus Prophet Muhammad (PBUH) made it obligatory for every Muslim – both male and female - to seek knowledge from 'cradle to the grave'. Note, some people perceive that Islam does not encourage women to be educated, and they are entirely wrong. We should not conceptualise a religion by observing the people of that religion in general as many people do not have correct knowledge and understanding about the religion, and many of them even don't practice religion. Many people do not have any formal study of religion.

We should instead learn the religion from its book (the Divine Scripture). In the case of Islam, we should consult the Qur'an and Hadith to understand this religion. However, we need to learn the right interpretations of the Qur'an and Hadith from the religious scholars with credentials and who work for reputed institutions. The wrong understandings of religion are causing a lot of problems in the world. The essence of religion is to unite human beings and promote harmony as they all have the same Creator. The importance of knowledge and the honour of the seeker of knowledge is explained by the following Hadith (*Sunan Abi Dawood, Vol. 4, Book of The Office of the Judge, Hadith 3634*).

> Narrated Kathir ibn Qays:
>
> Kathir ibn Qays said: I was sitting with AbudDarda' in the mosque of Damascus.
>
> A man came to him and said: AbudDarda, I have come to you from the town of the Messenger of Allah (Peace be upon him) for a tradition that I have heard you relate from the Messenger of Allah (Peace be upon him). I have come for no other purpose.
>
> He said: I heard the Messenger of Allah (Peace be upon him) say: If anyone travels on a road in search of knowledge, Allah will cause him to travel on one of the

roads of Paradise. The angels will lower their wings in their great pleasure with one who seeks knowledge, the inhabitants of the heavens and the Earth and the fish in the deep waters will ask forgiveness for the learned man. The superiority of the learned man over the devout is like that of the moon, on the night when it is full, over the rest of the stars. The learned are the heirs of the Prophets, and the Prophets leave neither dinar nor dirham, leaving only knowledge, and he who takes it takes an abundant portion.

The lights of knowledge unveil the truth and show us the path to the ultimate success of life. In the opening Surah of the Qur'an (1:6-7), Allah has taught humankind to seek guidance by asking for the right way, which leads to success.

Show us the straight way,

The way of those on whom You have bestowed Your Grace, those whose (portion) is not wrath, and who go not astray.

Then, in Surah Imran, Allah further explains that the path to success is the path that takes individuals to heaven.

Every soul shall have a taste of death: And only on the Day of Judgment shall you be paid your full recompense. Only he who is saved far from the fire and admitted to the garden will have attained the object (of life): For the life of this world is but goods and chattels of deception. (Qur'an 3:185)

Now, you may ask: what can I do to find the right path other than seeking guidance from God. Of course, we need to be sincere and humble in seeking guidance from God to find the right path to paradise. However, there are several ways to paradise that the Prophet (PBUH) has unveiled to humankind. I love to call it a strategy because we are more concerned about finding the right direction here. The strategy is simple. It is about (a) embarking on a journey in the pursuit of knowledge because knowledge will help us to distinguish right from the wrong and (b) once you find the right path hold on it, i.e., not only just acquire knowledge but also hold on to it. The scholars of Islam argues that when people meet in a room to learn the Qur'an with genuine sincerity, Shakina ('inner state of stillness in the heart' or the absolute tranquility of heart) descends as the Qur'an is the Divine guidance from our Creator and is the source of knowledge.

> Follow what you are taught by inspiration from thy Lord: there is no god but He: and turn aside from those who join gods with Allah. (Qur'an 6: 106)

Given that the Qur'an is the Divine message from God, the knowledge and teachings it encompasses are obligatory for all of humankind. The practical implication of the Qur'an has reflected through the life of the Prophet (PBUH).

> In a Hadith, Qatadah reported: I said, "O mother of the believers, tell me about the character of the Messenger of Allah, peace and blessings be upon him." Aisha said, "Have you not read the Quran?" I said, "O course!" Aisha

said, "Verily, the character of the Prophet of Allah was the Qur'an." (Sahih Muslim 746)

Thus, the life of the Prophet (PBUH) is an excellent source of knowledge to live a fulfilling life and be successful both in this world and the eternal world.

LEADERS ARE READERS

The discussions so far, have addressed the importance of learning and gaining knowledge. However, we often face some critical questions: How can we learn? Does knowledge come a formal university degree, only? Well, a good university degree will undoubtedly help us to acquire specialized knowledge, but obtaining the degree does not mark the end of our learning. I often tell my students that their real education begins after their graduation. In fact, a great deal of what we learn in university is "how to learn". While gaining specific knowledge, we also figure out the best ways each of us learns. This shapes our learning strategy. We need to work on our learning strategy throughout our life, as acquiring knowledge involves a lifelong commitment and quest. Finding the best approach to learn is obviously helpful. We all should become a lifelong learner if we want to grow. There are many ways we can acquire knowledge – observing, thinking, discussing, debating, problem–solving and reflecting. These are some of the means of learning. We can also learn from our life experiences. Nonetheless, a great way of learning and acquiring knowledge and keep growing is to make a habit of reading. You can take it as one of the most effective strategies to develop yourself. This is the mantra of a great leader. If we apply other tactics such as observing, thinking, discussing, debating, problem–solving and reflecting to better understand what we read, we can certainly learn and grow more effectively. Reading is the mantra of a great leader.

> "Today a reader, tomorrow a leader" Margaret Fuller

Reading opens up the way to become a leader, and good leaders never stop reading. The fortune 500 company CEOs read in an average of 60 books a year, and many of them use the 'App' or summaries to read as many books as possible. Through 'gatesnotes,' Bill Gates often shares the books he reads every year. When Bill Gates was the Chairman and CEO of Microsoft, every year, he used to keep aside two weeks to read the latest PhD thesis in the areas of science and innovation focusing on the development of new technologies. Reading was one of his competitive advantages as a leader. If we stop reading, we possibly stop learning, as this displays an attitude that we are not interested in learning. You may argue that we can learn from our life experiences – but if we are not interested in reading, we might not be keen to take lessons from our life experiences either. How many people have you come across who have made similar mistakes many times in their life? Possibly many, right? That's the point – if we are keen to learn, you will be a proactive learner. An active learner is likely to read and learn from others' experiences and worldviews. Reading is a formalised, organised, and a proactive way of acquiring knowledge. It has great importance in Islam as a way of seeking knowledge. When the man from Arabia, Muhammad was meditating inside 'cave Hira' at the 'Mountain Jabal al-Nour', the first command that came to him from the God and the Creator of the universe through Angel Gabriel was 'Iqra' meaning 'Read'. After saying twice, '*I cannot read*', Muhammad started reciting as the Angel Gabriel recited the following verses (Qur'an 96: 1-5):

1. Read: In the Name of your Lord who created.
2. Created man from a clot.
3. Read: And your Lord is the Most Generous.
4. He who taught by the pen.
5. Taught man what he never knew."

These five verses were the first revelation from God upon Prophet Muhammad (PBUH). The recitation of these verses was the beginning of his transformation. He became the Messenger of God. Therefore, the grand mission started with a monumental act of reading, putting Prophet Muhammad (PBUH) into a journey of seeking knowledge with three primary objectives:

1. To know his Creator;
2. To understand his mission on earth;
3. To bring humankind from darkness to light through communicating the Divine message of God and demonstrating its teachings through his art of living.

That was just the beginning, and we all know the rest! Muhammad (PBUH) became the final messenger of God and a leader with a legacy of leaving the highest number of followers in the world. His name is now followed by the phrase, "Peace Be Upon Him". Many of his followers copy even his lifestyle - the way he lived his life ranging from wearing clothing, keeping the beard, eating food, drinking water, treated people with utmost dignity to doing regular worships. The Divine message that was brought to humankind by Prophet Nuh, Abraham, Jesus, Moses (peace be upon them all) were completed through Prophet Muhammad (PBUH) – he was also called as a mercy to humankind, jinn and all those created by God.

> We sent you not, but as a Mercy for all creatures. (Qur'an 21:107)

But the point is simple: his transformation began with the act of reading in the name of his Lord Who created him. To further understand the significance of reading, it is reasonable to have a brief discussion of '*Iqra*' – the first Divine command that came to Prophet Muhammad (PBUH). '*Iqra*' is an Arabic word, which means 'read' according to *the translation of the Qur'an by* Pickthall, Shakir, Mohsin Khan. According to the Sahih International *translation*, 'Iqra' means 'recite'. Yusuf Ali has translated it as '*proclaim*'. Historically, we know that the then Arab world was far from the civilisation where women had no respect, the young girls were buried alive, and people used to worship idols that were created by themselves. The time was known as Jāhilīyah, i.e., the period of ignorance or barbarism (*Encyclopedia Britannica*). Allah showed Prophet Muhammad (PBUH) that the way to bring people from ignorance to light is to enlighten them with the knowledge so that they can know their Creator, which started by reading and reciting. According to Islamic scholars, one of the two dimensions of '*Iqra*' is a recitation from memory or by hearing another person. This has a connotation with understanding and propagation of the Divine message – i.e., learning and teachings of the Qur'an. Initially, Prophet Muhammad (PBUH) recited the verses of the Qur'an after hearing from Angel Gabriel. Afterword, he recited from his memory. This was then captured by his companions, who also read, recited, discussed, and contemplated to understand the inner meaning of the Divine words. However, it was indeed the mercy of Allah that Muhammad (PBUH) remembered and understood the Holy Qur'an (Qur'an 75: 16-17:

> 16. Move not thy tongue concerning the (Qur'an) to make haste therewith.
>
> 17. It is for Us to collect it and to promulgate it:
>
> 18. But when We have promulgated it, follow thou its recital (as promulgated):
>
> 19. Nay more, it is for Us to explain it (and make it clear):

The other dimension of '*Iqra*' is reading from a written text, which refers to reading the final message of God

(The Holy Qur'an) after it was compiled as a Holy Book.

> (It will be said to him:) "Read your (own) record: sufficient is your soul this day to make out an account against you." (Qur'an 17:14)

Thus, it is clear that reading has a profound impact on our lives, and this is one of the best ways of acquiring knowledge and enhancing our personal growth.

KNOWLEDGE: DIVINE VS SECULAR

At this point, it is necessary to address the question that we all have encountered many times in our life: *what kind of knowledge really matters?* In our quest to find the answer, let me invite you to ponder on the first five verses that were revealed to Prophet Muhammad (PBUH) once again (Quran 96:1-5).

1. Read: In the Name of your Lord who created.
2. Created man from a clot.
3. Read: And your Lord is the Most Generous.
4. He who taught by the pen.
5. Taught man what he never knew.

I believe, if you try to understand the significance of these verses through consulting their explanations drawing on viewpoints of different scholars of Qur'an, you will be able to find the answer yourself. In my quest of understanding the invaluable lessons drawn from these verses, the explanation of Qadhi (2015) has great significance. According to Qadhi (2015), the command *Read* mentioned in verse number 1 and verse number 3 refers to two types of knowledge.

The first *Read* in verses numbers 1 refers to sacred knowledge that allows us to know our Creator, the purpose of our life, and how we should live our life to be successful both here and hereafter (i.e., do's and don'ts in light of the Divine scripture). Qur'an and Hadith are the sources of sacred knowledge as Prophet Muhammad (PBUH), the final messenger of Allah, mentioned in his last sermon: "O People, no prophet or messenger will come after me and no new faith will be born. Reason well, therefore, O People, and understand words, which I convey to you. I am leaving you with the Book of God (the Qur'an) and my Sunnah (the lifestyle and the behavioral mode of the Prophet). If you follow them you will never go astray." (The Last Sermon of The Prophet Muhammad).

The second 'Read' in verse numbers 3 (linking to 4) refers to secular knowledge, which is captured through the use of the pen. Qadhi (2012) further argues that this worldly knowledge has also been taught to individuals by their Creator and includes several examples in support of his argument. For instance, Allah taught Adam (PBUH) the names (concepts) of all the things, which even the angels did not know (Qur'an 2: 31-33).

And He taught Adam the nature of all things; then He

> placed them before the angels, and said: "Tell me the nature of these if ye are right."
>
> They said: "Glory to You, of knowledge we have none, save what You have taught us: In truth it is You who art perfect in knowledge and wisdom."
>
> He said: "O Adam! Tell them their natures." When he had told them, Allah said: "Did I not tell you that I know the secrets of heaven and earth, and I know what ye reveal and what ye conceal?"

Quadhi (2012) goes on to say that Prophet Idrees (PBUH) was the first man to be taught by Allah to record the 'sounds' in writing. This is the origin of where the writing, painting, calligraphy, and printing have evolved. Allah taught Prophet Nuh (PBUH) how to build a ship, which eventually taught mankind to invent the modes of new transportation. Allah also taught Prophet Dawood (PBUH), how to make iron malleable for the use of humanity. It is evident that Allah – our Creator – is He who taught mankind both sacred (spiritual) and secular (worldly) knowledge, and various streams of human knowledge spring from the sacred knowledge. The knowledge individuals acquire is also the manifestation of intellect that Allah has instilled in people: *"And He taught Adam the names of all things" (Quran 2:31)*. Moreover, humankind can't know things beyond what Allah has enabled them to know. Have you not noticed that every one of us is different from each other, so is our intellectual ability? Newton is different from Einstein; Einstein is different from Shakespeare; Shakespeare is different from Socrates – just a few to mention. In the Qur'an, Allah has said the following.

> Allah. There is no god but He,-the Living, the Self-subsisting, Eternal. No slumber can seize Him nor sleep. His are all things in the heavens and on earth. Who is there can intercede in His presence except as He permits? He knows what (appear to His creatures as) before or after or behind them. Nor shall they compass anything of His knowledge except as He wills. His Throne doth extend over the heavens and the earth, and He feels no fatigue in guarding and preserving them for He is the Most High, the Supreme (in glory). (Qur'an 2: 255).

Qur'an also confirms that the creation of culture and language are also created by God:

> O mankind! We created you from a single (pair) of a male and a female, and made you into nations and tribes, that you may know each other (not that you may despise (each other). Verily the most honoured of you in the sight of Allah is (he who is) the most righteous of you. And Allah has full knowledge and is well acquainted (with all things). (Qur'an 49: 13)

While both sacred and secular knowledge are essential to living a better life, sacred (Divine) knowledge has a profound role in understanding:

1. The purpose of our life
2. Our relationship with our Creator
3. How we can succeed in life by using both sacred and secular knowledge.

Sacred knowledge also plays a profound role in *shaping*

our character by teaching us *ethics and morality* (good versus evil). What is good/ bad maybe subjective and people may have different opinions. So, the ultimate moral scale is the scale given by our Creator. The worldly knowledge, besides, uplifting our life and advancing the civilisation, also helps us to better understand the teachings of the Divine wisdom. Many discoveries have helped people to understand the message of the Qur'an in the light of science. In his seminal works, *"The Bible, the Qur'an and Science: The Holy Scriptures Examined in the Light of Modern Knowledge"*, Dr Maurice Bucaille explained how science helped him to understand the Divine scripture. Later, he became a Muslim. Seeking both kinds of knowledge is critical for developing wisdom and insights through which leaders create their third eye: the Gut. And this is important for every leader to function effectively.

THE APPLICATION OF KNOWLEDGE

There is no doubt that knowledge is power, but the potential of knowledge is realised when it is implemented. Knowledge does not matter unless we use it in the right way. Thus, the purpose of knowledge is to empower us to act in the most right and appropriate way possible. The following Hadith (*Sahih Al-Bukhari: Vol 1, Book 3, Hadith 79*) will shed light on this point.

Narrated by Abu Musa

> The Prophet said, "The example of guidance and knowledge with which Allah has sent me is like abundant rain falling on the earth, some of which was fertile soil that absorbed rain water and brought forth vegetation and grass in abundance. (And) another portion of it was hard and held the rain water and Allah benefited the people with it and they utilized it for drinking, making their animals drink from it and for irrigation of the land for cultivation. And) a portion of it was barren which could neither hold the water nor bring forth vegetation (then that land gave no benefits). The first is the example of the person who comprehends Allah's religion and gets benefit (from the knowledge) which Allah has revealed through me (the Prophets) and learns and then teaches others. The last example is that of a person who does not care for it and does not take Allah's guidance revealed through me (He is like that barren land.)"

The scholars say that the power of knowledge unleashes when knowledge becomes wisdom and allow us to understand things and gives us the ability to take the appropriate actions. For example, to lead a righteous life, we need to know Who our Creator is and His guidelines for us. Divine knowledge has the power to take an individual from darkness to light only if their understanding is translated into the right actions. At the end of the day, we will be judged by our Creator based upon our deeds.

> He Who created Death and Life, that He may try which of you is best in deed: and He is the Exalted in Might, Oft-Forgiving (Qur'an 67: 2)

Thus, the Qur'an reminds individuals about the importance of good deeds. However, if we want to do good deeds, we need to know what those are (i.e., the knowledge of the teachings of the Qur'an) and how we can accomplish them (i.e., the knowledge of Hadith). The following verse of the Qur'an explains that people who know and who don't know are not equal, and it is the knowledge of God that makes people humble and obedient to their Lord – the right knowledge leads to right actions (*Ilm leads to Amal*).

> Is one who is devoutly obedient during periods of the night, prostrating and standing [in prayer], fearing the Hereafter and hoping for the mercy of his Lord, [like one who does not]? Say, "Are those who know equal to those who do not know?" Only they will remember [who are] people of understanding. (Qur'an 39:9)

In other places in the Qur'an, Allah asks the believers to fear Him. Indeed, people with knowledge are fearful of their Lord.

> O you who believe! Fear Allah, and let every soul look to what (provision) He has sent forth for the tomorrow. Yea, fear Allah: for Allah is well-acquainted with (all) that you do. (Qur'an 59:18)

> And so amongst men and crawling creatures and cattle, are they of various colours. Those truly fear Allah, among His servants, who have knowledge: for Allah is Exalted in Might, Oft-Forgiving. (Qur'an 35:28)

This further emphasises the value of knowledge in Islam.

Knowledge is also essential for better leadership and management. People with knowledge are the doers - for knowledge enable them to do the right thing (leadership) in the right way (management). Seeking knowledge is an essential strategy in pursuing the ultimate vision of humankind (i.e., paradise). The following Hadith (Sunan Abu Dawood, Book 18, Hadith 28795) explains *three things* related to the knowledge that we need to manifest in our lives to gain the benefit of it.

> Narrated Abdullah ibn Amr ibn al-'As: The Prophet (Peace be upon him) said: Knowledge has three categories; anything else is extra; a precise verse, or an established sunnah (practice), or a firm obligatory duty.

We should never stop learning. When we stop learning, we stop growing. But to be more precise, we should not stop reading, which diminishes the real beauty of life. Make a habit of reading, and you will see you will be creating new worlds inside you which is beautiful. It will give you lights in your eyes, and you will see the world differently. You experience the joy of growing every day. It is a different experience - you can reveal life through lifelong learning, and reading is a great strategy. Often I ask my students a question: what is the difference between a person who can read and who cannot? Some of the answers I used to get are huge; no match; one is in the dark whereas the other is in the light; it's like night and day. Then I ask the second question: what is the difference between a person who cannot read and a person who can but does not? Most of the time, I have found that this question makes the point regarding the importance of reading, and my students get the message. I used to see some positive reactions among my students. As a leader, you might use this technique to encourage people working in your team. All of us have a moral responsibility to help others. When in doubt, do not hesitate to ask questions to those who know.

CASE STUDY

We are often too enthusiastic in telling stories of the movers and shakers of the world but shy to promote the unsung heroes, whose contributions are mostly unnoticed. People can certainly learn from reading the stories of iconic leaders. However, they often find it easier to relate to the life-stories of unsung heroes. *How many unsung heroes do you know who can inspire others to embark on a transformational journey?*

Let me introduce a naval Commodore. His name is Shafiul Bari. I believe his story will resonate with you. Shafiul got admission into a medical college to become a doctor, which was quite challenging in the context of Bangladesh. Becoming a doctor or an engineer was the dream profession in Bangladesh at that time. After a year of study, he was fascinated by the Navy. It was challenging to make a turn for a completely new career. However, Shafiul took the challenge and joined

Bangladesh Navy as a cadet on 01 January 1990 with the 90A batch. Although I knew him before, in the Navy, we found a new relationship: we were course mates. Our friendship renewed further, and eventually, he became one of my best friends. Shafiul developed a habit of reading during his time in medical college. He could read fast too, which gave him an advantage throughout his career. He was the first in our batch to do the specialisation course in Navigation and one of the first few to complete the Staff College. These are the two significant hurdles naval officers usually need to cross to have a smooth career. There is a saying in the Navy that *officers who are enthusiastic readers eventually become good leaders.* But I believe Shafiul was a good learner as well. Shafiul's habit of reading helped him crossing all the career hurdles in the Navy. He has an open mind. I never found him participating in any debate or discussion with a fixed mindset. This is a precious gift for any leader who really wants to learn and grow. We had hundreds of thought-provoking conversations, but in the end, our understanding of the topics and the perception of the worldview improved. We learned from each other. Shafiul is very inquisitive to know new things and get different perspectives. While I was in the Navy, we spent long hours reading books and articles and watching documentaries together and discussing various new ideas we came across to improve our understanding. This habit continued over the phone even after I left the Navy. One day I heard his wife was saying to my wife that we both are excellent listeners to each other. However, Shafiul was also keen to extend the arc of his knowledge domains from management, leadership, operational art, and maritime strategy to spirituality. He eventually became fascinated by the invaluable wisdom of the Qur'an, which illuminates lives and brings humankind from *the darkness of ignorance* to the *lights of awareness* at the heart of which is the consciousness of God. It was a blessing of God to find Shafiul as a friend and walk through the path between the domain of sacred and secular knowledge. More and more, our friends are joining the movement of lifelong learning. Recently we launched a discussion forum where some of our friends joined us to comprehend the real meaning of life through the lens of the Divine scripture and how we can bring our values to life. The team has members with a diverse background – a scientist from Silicon Valley and a senior leader from the World Food Programme.

> What can you learn from the story of two friends? Capture your thoughts and develop a plan to become a lifelong learner.

You have a choice to decide who are going to be your friends. It is better to have one friend who is hungry for knowledge than hundreds who are crazy for money, power, and image. It is better to have one friend who believes in you and let you believe in yourself. It is better to have one friend who has a pair of ears ready to hear the stories of your life. And if you get a few like them, you are part of a tribe who will protect you and create an environment for you to grow. When I was writing my previous book, The Purpose of Life: Understanding the Divine Scripture through the Lens of Leadership and Strategy, my friends, Bari read the whole book word for word and talked to me over the phone about his feelings. My other friends, Hafiz and Shahin, also read most of the chapters despite their busy schedule and gave their comments. My former Head of Department, Jonathan Groucutt, not only read the manuscript but also commented on every page for me to think and rethink. There is a saying that *you are defined by the five friends you spend most of your time with*. Be friendly with everyone. Help others and exchange smiles with the strangers. However, do not compromise in choosing your friends. Choose those who can help you, and you can help them in your quest to learn and grow. It will help you develop your third eye and experience the beauty of life. *What is the point of living if we don't know the meaning of life?*

LEADERSHIP IMPLICATION

To grow and let others grow, a leader needs to become a lifelong learner, seeking every opportunity to acquire knowledge. A leader who can coach his/ her team better, and can create a learning culture within his organisation, enjoy the competitive advantage. Knowledge and experience give people the third eye so they can see the world differently. As a good leader and a good follower, one needs to continue to seeking knowledge from all credible sources.

> In a Hadith – "Abu Huraira reported: The Messenger of Allah, peace and blessings be upon him, said, "The wise saying is the lost property of the believer, so wherever he finds it then he has a right to it." (Jami` at-Tirmidhi, Vol. 5, Book of Knowledge, Hadith 2687).

However, we need to remember that knowledge should make us humble rather than arrogant. Every time I read a journal article for my research, I learn a lot, but interestingly this learning lets me know how little I know from the vast amount of knowledge.

> The beauty of learning is to discover how little we know. Knowledge gives us confidence, but wisdom and insights save us from arrogance.

True leaders embark on a lifelong learning to stay relevant and effective. They also take their people along with them on this journey. It is the pursuit of knowledge, both Divine and useful worldly knowledge, that shape our eyes, minds and hearts so that we can see, think and feel differently. You can look through the window to see the world, but it is your knowledge that constructs the world in your mind. It is your third eye that determines what you see. Embark on a lifelong learning and enjoy the journey called life.

PART III

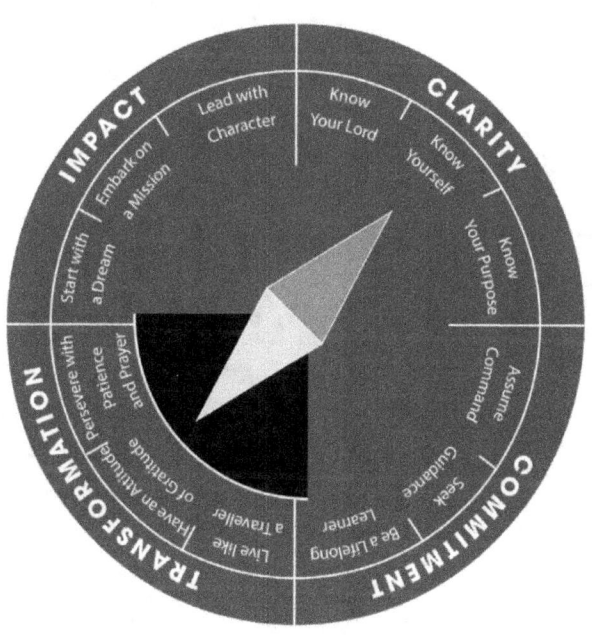

TRANSFORMATION

> Man cannot discover new oceans unless he has the courage to lose sight of the shore.
>
> Andre Gide

7

LIVE LIKE A TRAVELLER
Find Abundance in Less

During your journey through this world, another pointer of our 'leadership compass' is to develop a traveller-mind-set. A traveller is a person who wants to explore the world to seek unforgettable experiences. There are two kinds of travellers mentioned in the tourism and destination marketing literature. While some people see travelling as a way of escaping from the hardships and mundanity of everyday life, others take it as a means of seeking the meaning of life (Robledo and Batle, 2017) through exploring the wonders of the world and meeting with new people. Either way, the real travellers are mostly the experience seekers and are not too concerned about their possessions during travelling. It appears that the fewer their belongings (i.e. things they need to carry while travelling) are, the easier their travelling and the more enjoyable their experiences are. Travellers know that their stay in a particular place is just for a short while, and in most cases, the adventurous travellers carry only a backpack. A traveller-mind-set will allow us to experience the beauty of the creations of God while saving us from being overtaken by the materialistic world.

> He Who created the seven heavens one above another: no want of proportion will you see in the creation of (Allah) Most Gracious. So turn your vision again: see you any flaw? Again turn your vision a second time: (your) vision will come back to you dull and discomfited, in a state worn out. (Qur'an 67: 3-4)

Thus, we can focus on the far more important calling rather than indulge in a luxuries life. Developing a traveller-mind-set will help us realise the truth that we are in this world only for a short visit. We need to understand that the length of our time in this world is just for a while and we are nothing but travellers. Unless we can deeply realise this undeniable reality, we can be easily distracted by so many short-term priorities and forget the grand purpose of our life. The fact of the matter is our infinite life begins only after our death. Thinking about death is an effective tactic was to develop a traveller-mind-set and focus on the life hereafter. This reminds me once again the advice that Steve Jobs gave on 12th of June 2005 during his commencement address for the Standford University graduates. These fresh graduates were excited with loads of dreams to make a difference in the world, and Stanford understood there was no better choice than Steve Jobs to ignite their passion. Steve Jobs delivered a different kind of speech and told three stories of his life that would inspire anyone. One of his stories was on *death*, which I want to share with you here to make my point.

> "Remembering that I'll be dead soon is the most important tool I've ever encountered to help me make the big choices in life. Because almost everything — all external expectations, all pride, all fear of embarrassment or failure — these things just fall away in the face of death, leaving only what is truly important. Remembering that you are going to die is the best way I know to avoid the trap of thinking you have something to lose. You are already naked. There is no reason not to follow your heart... No one wants to die. Even people who want to go to heaven don't want to die to get there. And yet death is the destination we all share. No one has ever escaped it. And that is as it should be, because Death is very likely the single best invention of Life. It is Life's change agent. It clears out the old to make way for the new. Right now the new is you, but someday not too long from now, you will gradually become the old and be cleared away. Sorry to be so dramatic, but it is quite true. Your time is limited, so don't waste it living someone else's life." Steve Jobs

Steve Jobs suggests that thinking of death will make you do what matters in life. I just want to extend the horizon of life and encompass the next life, which decides the ultimate success or failure of our life. By this, I am not underestimating the importance of this life. I am instead underscoring the significance of our short stay on earth because how we live this life determines what we will get in the eternal life. We are born; we will die; and will be judged based upon our deeds in this life, measured against the guidelines/ criteria communicated to us by God through his messengers. The aim is to live life in a way so that we can be winners in the final judgment day. The objective is to save ourselves from the torment of hellfire and qualify ourselves for paradise. In the Qur'an, our Lord reminds us of this frequently.

> "O you who believe! save yourselves and your families from a fire whose fuel is men and stones, over which are (appointed) angels stern (and) severe, who flinch not (from executing) the commands they receive from Allah, but do (precisely) what they are commanded."(Qur'an 66:6)

We need to ponder on the message of God as His lieutenants on earth (Qur'an 2:30) rather than taking life easily and living without clarity of life's grand purpose. Developing a traveller-mid-set can help us transform the way we perceive life in this world and design a life that is aligned with our mission. It will allow us to realise the powerful principle: less is more (Draper, 2012), which was practised by many great people in the world. I am not saying that we should not pursue wealth at all in this world. I am merely inviting you to realise the length of our life in the world in comparison to the infinite life we are going to have after the *Day of Judgment* – of course, it matters to you only if you believe in the life hereafter, and you have your freedom to decide how you think. Every one of us has been created with intellect, and we are individually responsible for the choices we make after given the criteria for success. I only invite you to ponder that you should not fail in the never-ending life while pursuing this short worldly life. When compared to eternal life, our stay in this world is not even a journey we often take. However, I am not suggesting that you need to altogether leave everything in this world. Allah has not said that either. In the Qur'an, Allah has advised the individuals to seek his bounty (sustenance) after the prayer is over.

> And when the prayer is finished, then may you disperse through the land, and seek of the bounty of Allah and celebrate the praises of Allah often (and without stint): that you may prosper. (Qur'an 62:10)

The point I want to make is to pursue the grand purpose of life while seeking the bounty of God and making an honest living. The reality is money alone does not matter unless it creates meaning. But often we see many of us run after wealth and forget the most precious things in life: *our responsibilities to our Creator and His creations*. This is why our Creator has reminded us of this through His Divine message. Surah At-Takathur of the Holy Qur'an (102:1-8) is an excellent reminder for human beings, particularly for those who have forgotten their Lord and the grand purpose of life while competing for wealth with one another despite knowing that we are merely the trustees of our wealth and we will not be able to take it with us into our graves.

1. The mutual rivalry for piling up (the good things of this world) diverts you (from the more serious things),
2. Until you visit the graves.
3. But nay, you soon shall know (the reality).
4. Again, you soon shall know!
5. Nay, were you to know with certainty of mind, (you would beware!)
6. You shall certainly see hellfire!
7. Again, you shall see it with certainty of sight!
8. Then, shall you be questioned that day about the joy (you indulged in!).

This Surah of the Qur'an has a profound message for all of us from our Creator. While explaining this Surah, the *Islamic Scholars* focus on two *Arabic phrases* used in the Surah: '*Ilm al Yaqeen*' and '*Aynul Yaqeen*'. The Arabic word '*Yaqeen*' means 'certainty'. This will help us explain these two phrases. '*Ilm al Yaqeen*' means '*certainty of mind*' whereas '*Aynul Yaqeen*' means '*certainty of sight*'. These two phrases differentiate between leaders and non-leaders from short-term vs long-term perspective. Leaders are those who can see the future and can make the right choice. Leaders usually can see beyond the horizon (the future) through their knowledge (intuition/ power of vision) that shapes their worldview. In contrast, those who can't see far, see things with their 'sights' – i.e. their eyes, and there is a limit on how far we can see with our eyes. This reminds me that when many people and organisations saw a world market for only five computers, Bill Gates could see that every desk in the world needed a computer. In this Surah, Allah has warned humankind to refrain from the unhealthy competition of pilling up wealth, which keeps them away from far more significant things in life. Allah states that if individuals use their intellect wisely, they can realise the importance of the life hereafter and be successful through saving them from the torment of hellfire. Thus, *'Ilm al Yaqeen' or 'certainty of mind/knowledge'* helps us to focus on the long-term rather than be short-sighted. Indeed, if we cannot think of death and cannot see our grave, we really are not seeing far. However, if we can see our grave, it is easy for us to respond to the grand purpose of our life. This life is for tests. We need to make the most of our time and pass the tests for a better life hereafter. Eternal life is better than the worldly life for the believer. However, most of us tend not to understand this reality. In the Qur'an, Allah states what attracts people.

> Fair in the eyes of men is the love of things they covet: women and sons; heaped-up hoards of gold and silver; horses branded (for blood and excellence); and (wealth of) cattle and well-tilled land. Such are the possessions of this world's life; but in nearness to Allah is the best of the goals (to return to) (Qur'an 3:14)

However, in reality, none of the things mentioned in this verse (except the nearness of our Lord) will benefit us in any way after our death if we do not use them properly.

This reminds me of three *final wishes* of *Alexander*. Alexander has a unique position in history as a famous military commander. None could defeat him in any battle. Then before his death, he could realise the true meaning of life. He expressed his final three wishes to his generals, wanting them to carry out these wishes after his death.

1. *First,* his physicians should carry his coffin.
2. *Second,* his treasure should be scattered along the path while taking his coffin to the grave.
3. *Third,* his two hands need to put outside his coffin so that everyone can see them.

When his most favourite general asked the reason, with a deep breath, he explained the reasons.

1. *First,* everyone would realise that physicians cannot do anything in the face of death.
2. *Second,* people would know that even Alexander could not take wealth to his grave. After death, wealth has no value at all to the dead person.
3. *Third,* people would see that even Alexander was leaving the world empty-handed.

Alexander finished explaining and left the world. This story helps us understand the message of Surah At-Takathur: the value of all that we strive in life. Surah Al Haqqah (Qur'an 69: 25-37) gives us the same message.

25. And he that will be given his record in his left hand, will say: "Ah! Would that my record had not been given to me!
26. "And that I had never realised how my account (stood)!
27. "Ah! Would that (death) had made an end of me!

28. "Of no profit to me has been my wealth!
29. "My power has perished from me!"
30. (The stern command will say): "Seize you him, and bind you him,
31. "And burn you him in the blazing fire.
32. "Further, make him march in a chain, of which the length is seventy cubits!
33. "This was he that would not believe in Allah Most High.
34. "And would not encourage the feeding of the needy!
35. "So no friend hath he here this day.
36. "Nor has he any food except the corruption from the washing of wounds,
37. "Which none do eat but those in sin."

While people are so interested in the worldly life, Allah goes on telling that He has far better things than those:

> Say, "Shall I inform you glad tidings far better than those? For the righteous are gardens in the nearness to their Lord, with revers flowing beneath; in it is their eternal home; with companions pure (and holy) and the good pleasure of Allah. For in Allah's sight are (all) His servants – (Qur'an 3:15)

In summary, I wanted to stress the strategic implication of developing a traveller-mind-set as leaders so that they cannot only guide themselves but also their people in the right direction. Having a traveller's mindset will help us prioritise between short-term and long-term goals. It will help us realise that the ultimate success of humankind depends upon the outcome in the eternal life, which by length is incomparable with such a short life on earth. It will let us ask the profound question: what does really matter? Let me finish this chapter with a case study.

CASE STUDY

Life is a short journey, and we are merely travellers. We all have a choice to make. Developing a traveller-mindset can help us to live happily. "The secret of happiness is not found in seeking more, but in developing the capacity to enjoy less," said the Greek philosopher Socrates. We do not need much to be happy in life. The memories of my midshipman training onboard a Frigate where I found abundance in less is still fresh in my mind. This was an unforgettable experience, teaching me that the cornerstone of happiness is laid on relationships that centre around compassion and empathy for fellow human beings. This is the type of relationship that sailors share among themselves while they grow up as leaders in the limited spaces of the worships. The sense of brotherhood let them sacrifice for the fellow members of the team and die for the nation.

On-board the ship, we were a total of ten midshipmen, living in a small cabin. I can still vividly see the faces of every member: Arif Ahmed Mustafa (now a Commodore), Saifur Rahman (now a Captain), Abdullah Al Maksus (now a Captain), Mokhlesur Rahman (now no more with us in this world), Aminur Rahman (now settled with a corporate career), Toriqul Islam (now a Captain), Mainul Islam Sarker (now a Commander), Reza Shah Pahlabi (now a Commander), Sayeed

Mahmud (now a Captain) and Nazam Uddin (now Lieutenant Commander). After six months, the midshipmen from our senior batch were commissioned and left the ship for further professional training. Then two more midshipmen – Joynal Abedin (now a Captain) and Abdul Latif (now running his own business in the garment sector) joined the team. Everyone had one bunk bed and a small drawer-type locker to keep uniforms and a few civilian clothes. Everyone had a kitbag to store a few extra things not used regularly. We used to keep our kitbags in the ship's store, as our cabin had no space to accommodate those. Although we had very few things, we were the happiest people in the world. This was the time I learnt the art of finding abundance in less and could be happy only with a kitbag and a bunk bed.

I remember we all enjoyed a wonderful time living together in a small cabin, which taught us self-discipline and people-centric leadership. Every night, before sleeping, we used to talk about numerous things that happened during the day. Living so many people together was an excellent opportunity to understand each other and develop empathy. To be able to sacrifice for others with a smiling face was possibly the best things Navy has taught us. I can vividly remember about one night when the ship was at sea, and I was doing the middle watch (12 to 4 am), working on the bridge of the Frigate and supporting the Officer of the Watch (OOW). It was winter, and the weather was excellent. The sea was calm, and there was a full moon in the sky. I never had the chance to experience the beauty of the full moon standing on the deck of a ship. It was a wonderful feeling. I was lost in the depth of my fantasy. Experiencing the beauty of the world and forgot about everything. There was no song playing on the background, but there was a melody in my heart, whispering to me that to be happy in life, we only need a sky with a full moon and be surrounded with people who you can trust - people who can sacrifice for each other.

Once, during a weather-warning signal, the ship was going to the shelter station. On the way, we encounter an extremely rough sea. I was feeling seasickness, struggling to stand on the bridge. Many sailors were vomiting, but we had a mission to take the ship to a safe shelter. That night, my coursemate, Saifur Rahman, sacrificed his sleep at night to help me with my watch. Saifur is known as a man with a big heart for his enormous empathy and compassion for others. Saifur is second to none in running the operation of a naval base. He led a Cadet College, which became one of the best institutions in the country, and he recognised as the best Principal in the country in 2015. He was also awarded medals in his operational excellence in both Navy and Coast Guard. Recently, I had an opportunity to witness him leading his people while having a conversation sitting in his Captain's office. When he was briefing his teams, I could feel how passionate he was with his role and satisfied with his job. I could learn that if leaders are not passionate about what they do, they cannot motivate their people. You cannot fake authenticity. Living with many people together and learning to sacrifice for each other, reshaped my perception of happiness and leadership. I believe through developing compassion and empathy for humankind, we can find real happiness.

We need a pair of compassionate eyes to notice the beauty of life and a loving heart to feel the blessings of God showering upon us every moment. Things that can make us truly happy are priceless and does not cost much - mostly free.

It is free to see the full moon in a moonlit night. It is free to walk through a beautiful park and enjoy the natural beauty. Happiness is not found in the things we have. It comes as we learn to appreciate what we have. A life of abundance is not created by how many things we have. It is produced by how we understand the value of whatever we have. If we learn how to live like a traveller, we may as well learn how to find abundance in less. That's life – simple and easy. Very often, we make our lives difficult. While visiting Bangladesh last time, I meet my school friend, Muhammad Ali, who dedicated all his time staying with me, bringing our old memories to life. There was no anxiety in his eyes. At one point in our conversation, he told me that there are so many species created by God, but it is only the humankind who are the best in knowledge and skills but worry the most.

And [remember] when your Lord proclaimed, 'If you are grateful, I will surely increase you [in favor]; but if you deny, indeed, My punishment is severe.

(Qur'an 14: 7)

8

HAVE AN ATTITUDE OF GRATITUDE
Focus Your Eyes on the Prize

Have you ever thought about what if you were born as another species other than a human being? Is it not enough for us to be grateful to our Creator that He has created us as human and given us the intellect and free will? Allah mentions His blessings for the humankind in the Qur'an.

> If you would count up the favours of Allah, never would you be able to number them: for Allah is Oft-Forgiving, Most Merciful. (Qur'an 16:18)

When we cannot even finish counting the blessings of Allah upon us, how should we respond to His mercy for us? Yes, you guessed it right. Being grateful. Our lives, health, hearing, sight, feeling – all are the mercy of God, but human beings usually do not appreciate and fail to show their gratitude.

> It is He Who has created for you (the faculties of) hearing, sight, feeling and understanding: little thanks it is you give! (Qur'an 23:78)

Have you ever had the opportunity to think that the rest of God's creations are for the service of humankind, and we are making use of them? Read a few verses from Surah An-Naba of the Qur'an and look around. I believe you will be able to feel a sense of gratitude to realise how our Lord has designed this world for our living.

> Have We not made the earth a resting place? And the mountains as stakes? And We created you in pairs. And made your sleep [a means for] rest. And made the night as clothing. And made the day for livelihood. And constructed above you seven strong [heavens]. And made [therein] a burning lamp. And sent down, from the rain clouds, pouring water. That We may bring forth thereby grain and vegetation. And gardens of entwined growth. (Qur'an 78: 6-16)

Imagine what would be the condition if we had to pay for the oxygen we are breathing? Those who had to use ventilator during COVID-19 would understand it better. Every aspect of our life is a manifestation of the unlimited mercy of our Lord. Now one of the most valuable questions is how we should reciprocate to our Lord for the blessings we are living with every moment of our life? Our Creator is Self-Sufficient and does not need anything from us. Instead, we need Him in every aspect of our lives. Thus, the most sensible way of responding to the blessings we are enjoying every moment of our lives is to have an attitude of gratitude. As we have discussed before we can manifest the purpose of our life by being grateful and thankful to our Lord. However, this should not be limited to verbal declaration only. Instead, we need to demonstrate our gratitude to our Lord through our works. To show our appreciation and obedience, we should also submit to our Creator and worship Him, as He is the One and Only worthy of our worship, and that is the grand purpose of our life. The Islamic scholars state that showing gratitude or being grateful makes us humble to our Lord, which is both a form of prayer and a condition for worship. Showing gratitude is a requirement for the contentment of the heart. In Surah Al-Luqman, Allah states the importance of gratitude so that mankind can take lessons and be grateful and successful.

> We bestowed (in the past) wisdom on Luqman: "Show (your) gratitude to Allah." Any who is (so) grateful does so to the profit of his own soul: but if any is ungrateful, verily Allah is free of all wants, worthy of all praise. (Qur'an 31: 12)

Pondering on this verse, we can understand that being grateful and thankful to Allah and appreciating life – as it is – has a positive impact on our soul. Although there are millions of reasons for every one of us to be happy, many of us only see things that make us hopeless. This means there is a tremendous need for us to learn to focus on things that we should be grateful for. The art of being thankful is to compare us with those who have less than what we have. I am sure whatever may be our situation, we will find many people who have far less than us.

Perhaps, many of us have heard the story of a man who did not have a pair of shoes, and he was distraught with his life. However, the perception of his life changed when he saw another man without any leg. This is not just a story – this is something to ponder on. We could be one of those who are living in the war zone. We could be one of the many children in the world who go to sleep being hungry. We could be one of those children who have lost their parents. Thus, we should be grateful to our Creator for His uncountable blessings upon us.

Think about water. Do we make it ourselves? We all know that without water, we will not be able to survive, but we may not have the opportunity to realise this fact. If you were to fast for over eighteen hours during a hot summer, you might have understood what a big blessing and mercy of God that He has made the provision of water for us.

> Nor are the two bodies of flowing water alike – the one palatable, sweet, and pleasant to drink, and the other, salty and bitter. Yet from each (kind of water) do you eat flesh fresh and tender, and you extract ornaments to wear; and you see the ships in it that plough the waves, that you may

seek (thus) of the bounty of Allah that you may be grateful. (Qur'an 35: 12)

Learning to notice the countless mercy of God will help us to be grateful, and there is a direct correlation between gratitude and happiness. This is also supported by research in positive psychology. Allah wants His creations to be thankful. Being grateful is one of the ways to get more and more blessings and mercy from Him. There are many verses in the Qur'an that underscores the benefits of being grateful.

> And [remember] when your Lord proclaimed, 'If you are grateful, I will surely increase you [in favor]; but if you deny, indeed, My punishment is severe. (Qur'an 14: 7)

The spiritual implication of this verse is that if we genuinely become grateful to our Lord, Allah will increase His blessings upon us. When we develop an attitude of gratitude, we can see the world differently. Qur'an (1:1-7) teaches human beings to be grateful to their Lord and seek His guidance.

1. In the name of Allah, Most Gracious, Most Merciful.
2. Praise be to Allah, the Cherisher and Sustainer of the worlds;
3. Most Gracious, Most Merciful;
4. Master of the Day of Judgment.
5. You do we worship, and Your aid we seek.
6. Show us the straight way,
7. The way of those on whom You have bestowed Your Grace, those whose (portion) is not wrath, and who go not astray.

The beginning of the Surah: *'praise and thanks be to Allah'* shows that gratitude has a significant implication in our life. It is reasonable that we can only praise and thank our Lord when we are pleased with our lives. This Surah starts with the teaching of accepting our life by focusing our eyes on the enormous prizes of life and be thankful to our Lord. This Surah also shows us that it is the guidance (*show us the straight path*) that only comes from our Lord and is the best mercy.

While being grateful to our Lord brings significant wellbeing to us both here and hereafter, ingratitude has a significant adverse impact on our life. It not only leaves us in a state of hopelessness but also brings the wrath of Allah. Thus, the scholars of Islam have argued that 'gratitude' ('Shukr' in Arabic) has a connotation with the 'faith' ('Iman' in Arabic) and is an attribute of the believers. An attitude of gratitude also helps us to live with contentment.

LEADERSHIP IMPLICATION

There is also a profound implication of gratitude in the way we lead as a leader. Often, leaders become more concerned about their authority and position of power. Instead of serving their people, they become more interested in holding their ranks and titles so that they can enjoy several facilities. There are many examples of these leaders in the world. There are very few examples of good leaders who are really driven by the opportunity to serve their people. If we carefully, think about the inherent reasons behind these moral decay of the leaders, we can see that they are not happy with what they have and pursue more and more for their own. Thus, developing an attitude of gratitude not only help us to be pleased with serenity but also focus on the interest of the people we lead. That is when leaders make a real impact.

> "Gratitude makes sense of our past, brings peace for today, and creates a vision for tomorrow." Melody Beattie

> Patience is not simply the ability to wait - it's how we behave while we're waiting.
>
> Joyce Meyer

9

PERSEVERE WITH PATIENCE AND PRAYER
Transform through Struggles

A common question often asked by many people regarding the life of humankind on earth is why Adam and Eve (peace be upon them) were expelled from heaven. Some people think this was a punishment for their sins. They argue that as Satan made them eat fruits from a forbidden tree, Allah expelled them from heaven. However, the Qur'an clearly explains that men are God's lieutenants (i.e. vicegerent) on earth, and this was part of God's grand plan:

> Behold, your Lord said to the angels: "I will create a vicegerent on earth." They said: "Will you place therein

> one who will make mischief therein and shed blood?- whilst we do celebrate Your praises and glorify Your holy (name)?" He said: "I know what you know not." (Qur'an 2:30)

This honour of God's vicegerent on earth was given to human beings amongst all His creations. With the reputation, comes responsibility.

> "...On earth will be your dwelling-place and your means of livelihood - for a time." (Qur'an 2:36)

While the purpose of life is to worship (pray) God (Qur'an 51:56), this life is a testing place for humankind (Qur'an 67:2).

> Do men think that they will be left alone on saying, "We believe", and that they will not be tested? (Qur'an 29:2)

This verse of the Qur'an tells us that the mere verbal utterance of the declaration of faith is not enough as everyone can do that. The real faith is judged through tests, and Allah will test human beings. Allah values the piety of the individuals, which is manifested by the quality of their work. In another verse, Allah states that humankind will be judged for their deeds on earth.

> [He] who created death and life to test you [as to] which of you is best in deed - and He is the Exalted in Might, the Forgiving – (Qur'an 67: 2)

Therefore, it is further established that human beings, during their time on earth, will be judged (tested) by

Allah, who is the Owner of the Day of Judgment. Allah will reward them for their good deeds. No account will be taken of the colour of their skin, family background, social status and so on.

WHY SUFFERINGS

One of the most common questions that I often hear – especially from those who struggle to believe in the existence of God is why there are so many sufferings in this worldly life. There are stories all over the world that will bring tears in anyone's eyes. However, human beings are designed in a way that they are transformed through hardships and sufferings. It is the hardships and sufferings that help us develop ourselves. How can we feel the purity of our character if our character is never put to the test? The Qur'an has narrated the stories of 25 prophets (peace be upon them all) of God. Prophets are known to be the best people of their time and role models for humankind. All the prophets went through stringent tests, which transformed them into a true worshipper of God and developed their character, making them the best and exemplary people of their times. However, we most often see that many people fail to transform themselves during the time of difficulties and compromise with their integrity and character. When I was going through the tough naval training as an officer cadet, I came across two famous sayings: "train hard, fight easy." and "when the going gets tough, the tough get going." There are people whose character develops as they go through the struggles of life, and there is honourable mention of them in the Qur'an (2: 155-156).

> Be sure we shall test you with something of fear and hunger, some loss in goods or lives or the fruits (of your toil), but give glad tidings to those who patiently persevere,
>
> Who say, when afflicted with calamity: "To Allah we belong, and to Him is our return" -

These people know that whatever may be their sufferings, these are only for the time being because their life on earth is just a tiny fraction in comparison to the never-ending eternal life. Moreover, we all know everything in life changes, and so does our sufferings. Thus, in the above verse, Allah states that these people, when facing pain, say: "To Allah we belong, and to Him is our return". This not only develops their character but also increases their faith and reliance upon their Lord. In the Qur'an, Allah has clearly stated that He does not give any burden to his servants that they cannot bear, and our tests can be managed through the capabilities provided to us by our Lord.

> On no soul does Allah place a burden greater than it can bear. It gets every good that it earns, and it suffers every ill that it earns. (Pray:) "Our Lord! Condemn us not if we forget or fall into error; our Lord! Lay not on us a burden like that which You did lay on those before us; Our Lord! Lay not on us a burden greater than we have strength to bear. Blot out our sins, and grant us forgiveness. Have mercy on us. You are our protector; Help us against those

who stand against faith." (Qur'an 2:286)

Thus, facing the difficulties with the right spirit is a manifestation patience. There is a promise from Allah in the Qur'an that every difficulty comes with relief.

> So, verily, with every difficulty, there is relief. Verily, with every difficulty there is relief. (Qur'an 94: 5-6)

How to Deal with Suffering?

In the Qur'an, Allah not only confirms that we will be tested but also teaches us invaluable strategies to deal with those tests and sufferings of life: (a) patient perseverance, and (b) prayer. This is the ultimate recipe for transformation and becoming successful.

> O you who believe! seek help with patient perseverance and prayer: for Allah is with those who patiently persevere. (Qur'an 2:153)

The verses mentioned above has an important lesson for the humankind. This verse implies that we should never lose hope and always believe that through patient perseverance and prayer, we can overcome any difficulty and achieve any success. In this verse, Allah has not mentioned patience or perseverance or prayer alone - instead, combined all of them: 'patient perseverance' and 'prayer'. Thus, to deal with difficulties and to achieve success, this verse teaches some strategies: (a) We should continue to persevere; (b) We should remain patient, hopeful, and not give up; and (c) We should continue to rely upon God through prayer and never lose our faith upon Him.

The word 'patient perseverance' also teaches us that success may not be an immediate result of our perseverance. We need to be patient while trying and never lose faith in Allah. We should never be hopeless and should never stop praying and trying. Without patience, it is challenging to continue to persevere.

While talking about the virtue of patience (Sabr in Arabic), Menk (2011) mentioned about different facets of patience (Sabr), which are forbearance, endurance, steadfastness, perseverance, and restraint. Menk (2011) further focused on three kinds of patience.

The first kind of patience comes in the form of endurance that requires obeying the commands of Allah. For example, military training, which involves a lot of patience to complete. However, once you complete this training, you will be transformed into a different person. The second kind of patience is needed to abstain from the prohibitions of Allah. The third kind of patience is needed to accept the decrees of Allah during the time of calamities.

Throughout the Qur'an, Allah unveils the stories of His messengers. The way they demonstrated patient perseverance during difficulties teaches us valuable leadership lessons. Prophet Ayyub (PBUH) was one of the fortunate men of his time. He had cattle and crops, many children, and beautiful houses. He enjoyed all these blessings of his Lord for many years of his life. Then Allah decided to test him and took everything from him. All his children died one after another. The test did not stop there. He further suffered from terrible skin disease, and the condition was such that he had to live alone at one edge of the neighbourhood with no one to treat him except his wife. The situation got so severe that his wife had to work for people to earn money so that they could merely survive. Still, Prophet Ayyub (PBUH) did not stop remembering his God. He did not even complain, which is mentioned in the Qur'an.

> And (remember) Job, when He cried to his Lord, "Truly distress has seized me, but You are the Most Merciful of those that are merciful." So We listened to him: We removed the distress that was on him, and We restored his people to him, and doubled their number, - as a grace from Ourselves, and a thing for commemoration, for all who serve Us. (Qur'an 21: 83-84)

There is profound teaching for human beings and for the leaders in the story of Prophet Ayyub (PBUH) about how we need to deal with the sufferings in our lives – particularly when we are tested. The beautiful words and tone of Prophet Ayyub's (PBUH) supplication to his Lord - *"Truly distress has seized me, but You are the Most Merciful of those that are merciful"* – explain how patient he was at the most challenging time of his life. From the story of Prophet Ayyub (PBUH), we need to learn that he was extremely grateful to his Lord even in the hardest times of his life. That should be the character of a believer and a good leader. However, many of us are not grateful to our Lord during the best times of our lives. This story should inspire us to develop a character like Prophet Ayyub (PBUH) and overcome the adversities of life with gratitude, patient perseverance and prayer.

LEADERSHIP IMPLICATION

Patience is an invaluable attribute of a leader. All great leaders – from ancient times to the modern-days demonstrate their patience to achieve great things. Stated in the Qur'an, the story of Prophet Yunus (PBUH) also teaches us a beautiful lesson about the importance of patience in leadership. He was appointed as a leader of his time with the honour of being the messenger of God. When Prophet Yunus (PBUH) called the people of Nineveh (near Mosul in northern Iraq) with the message of God, they kept on rejecting his message. This frustrated him, and at some point, he lost his patience and left these people with anger and eventually boarded a ship. The ship encountered a storm, and people on-board were at risk of drowning due to heavy loads. To lighten the load, they drew lots to choose someone to be thrown off the ship. Although Prophet Yunus (PBUH) lost the draw three times, they did not want him to be thrown. But Prophet Yunus (PBUH) chose to do so himself. Qur'an (37: 139 – 142) mentions about it.

> So also was Jonah among those sent (by Us).

> When he ran away (like a slave from captivity) to the ship (fully) laden,
>
> He (agreed to) cast lots, and he was condemned:
>
> Then the big fish did swallow him, and he had done acts worthy of blame.

As Prophet Yunus (PBUH) lost his patience, Allah tested him inside three levels of darkness: the *darkness of the night,* the *darkness of sea* (underwater), and the *darkness of the belly of a big fish*. This is the moment Prophet Yunus (PBUH) could realise his mistake and seek forgiveness to his Lord through a beautiful supplication.

> And remember Dhu'n – Nun, when he departed in wrath: he imagined that We had no power over him! But he cried through the depths of darkness, "There is no god but You: glory to You; I was indeed wrong!" So We listened to him: and delivered him from distress: and thus do We deliver those who have faith. (Qur'an 21: 87-88)

The story of Prophet Yunus (PBUH) teaches us two vital leadership lessons.

First, leaders should neither lose their patience nor leave their people no matter how adverse the situation is. Second, humankind, whether in a position of leader or a follower, is likely to make mistakes. However, as soon as they realise their mistake, they should seek forgiveness of their Lord. Leaders with faith should never lose hope from the mercy of their Lord even they are in the three levels of darkness. The general teachings of the story for the humankind at large are as follows:

1. We need to be patient and hopeful in every phase of our life;
2. We need to repent for our mistakes and seek the forgiveness of Allah as much as we can;
3. We should consistently remember Him and glorify His Highness.

> Had it not been that he (repented and) glorified Allah, He would certainly have remained inside the fish till the day of resurrection. But We cast him forth on the naked shore in a state of sickness, And We caused to grow, over him, a spreading plant of the gourd kind. And We sent him (on a mission) to a hundred thousand (men) or more. And they believed; so We permitted them to enjoy (their life) for a while. (Qur'an 37: 143-148)

Keeping patience in the time of calamity is not an easy task. However, we can always try to employ some strategies that can help us to develop this quality. One approach is to focus on those who are facing difficult challenges and be grateful for our own condition. Often, the tests of life are indeed good for us as these help us realise our mistakes, seek repentance, develop empathy for less fortunate people, and be nearer to our Lord.

> In a Hadith, Anas ibn Malik reported: The Prophet, peace and blessings be upon him, said, "All of the children of Adam are sinners, and the best sinners are those who repent." (Sunan al-Tirmidhī 2499)

The other approach is to think of the blessings of God

that we have already enjoyed. For example, Prophet Ayyub (PBUH) reflected on his good days, which helped him remain patient and grateful during his adverse times. There was a moment in the life of the last Prophet, Muhammed (PBUH) when no message from Allah came to him for about six months. During this period, some people mocked at him, saying that his Lord has forsaken him. But the Prophet (PBUH) did not lose his patience and hope. Then the following Surah Ad-Duhaa (Qur'an 93:1-11) was revealed.

1. By the glorious morning light,
2. And by the night when it is still,-
3. The Guardian-Lord has not forsaken you, nor is He displeased.
4. And verily the hereafter will be better for you than the present.
5. And soon will your Guardian-Lord give you (that with which) you shall be well-pleased.
6. Did He not find you an orphan and give you shelter (and care)?
7. And He found you wandering, and He gave you guidance.
8. And He found you in need, and made you independent.
9. Therefore, treat not the orphan with harshness,
10. Nor repulse the petitioner (unheard);
11. But the bounty of the Lord - rehearse and proclaim!

Through this Surah not only Allah taught his last Messenger Muhammed (PBUH) great lessons but also drew a pearl of significant wisdom for human beings – His vicegerents, His lieutenant on earth as to how to navigate our lives with patient perseverance and prayer.

In this Surah, Allah has used two beautiful metaphors to denote the phases of life – ups and downs.

1. 'The glorious morning light' (verse 1)
2. 'The night when it is still' (verse 2)

Every one of us becomes depressed in times of adversity, but this Surah brings the message of hope, reminding us to be mindful of our good times and carry on with absolute faith in our Creator. The stillness of night makes us feel that we are indeed forsaken. A temporary hardship is a preparation for the daylight and never goes in vain. Indeed through difficulties, individuals are transformed. It is the tests and turbulence of life through which individuals grow. It is the struggles and unease of life that make us go beyond our comfort zone, not only opening up the doors of opportunities but also helping us develop exemplary character. Thus, our struggles should never be seen as a punishment - instead, a chance to grow.

The appearance of the daylight shows that the mercy of Allah is on the way, which will vanish the darkness of the night, and we need to learn to persevere, be patient and wait. The life of Prophet Muhammed (PBUH) metaphorically relates to all of us, and we can draw lessons from his life experience both as a leader and as a human. He was never impatient. He was an orphan, and Allah found him shelter (verse 6); he was given guidance when people were deeply involved in false worship (verse 7); he was poor, but Allah made him independent (verse 8). However, every difficulty of his life came to an end as a result of his patient perseverance. To accomplish the grand mission of spreading the message of Allah throughout his life, he demonstrated patience, perseverance, and gratitude. Despite living a righteous life as the messenger of Allah, he always asked for the forgiveness of Allah. All the difficulties of his life helped him to be the person he became: the noblest man ever born. His character was his primary charisma, attracting people from all walks of life towards him and towards Islam.

Surah Ad Duhaa also teaches us a great lesson on faith, which is interlinked with the two virtues of great leaders: patience and perseverance. These two lessons are in verses number 3 and 4, respectively. We can relate this to our lives as well. The significance of these two verses are: (a) when we are passing through difficult times, there is no reason to believe that God has forsaken us and He is displeased with us, and (b) the hereafter will be better for us than the present. If we really hold on to the teachings of these two verses, it will become easier for us to be patient and persevere in achieving the greater mission of life. Thus, everything in the life of a believer is a beautiful gift. According to a Hadith reported by Suhaib, the Messenger of Allah (PBUH) said:

> "Wondrous is the affair of the believer for there is good for him in every matter and this is not the case with anyone

> except the believer. If he is happy, then he thanks Allah and thus there is good for him, and if he is harmed, then he shows patience and thus there is good for him." (Sahih Muslim 2999)

This Hadith teaches us that the greatest blessings of faith help us to reflect on the fact that both ease and hardships are good for us. It is the hardships and tests that help us to get back on track in our journey to the ultimate success of life. In the Qur'an, Allah mentions the excellent advice that Luqman (PBUH) gave to his son.

> O my son! Establish regular prayer, enjoin what is just, and forbid what is wrong: and bear with patient constancy whatever befall you; for this is firmness (of purpose) in (the conduct of) affairs. (Qur'an 31:17 -19)

CASE STUDY

Struggling is an opportunity to grow and develop our character. Once, I was working within an insurance company in London. This was a hard time in my life. It was challenging to manage my family with only one job. I convinced my boss to spare me for two days a week for doing a teaching job. This helped me to make some extra money to support my family. I covered up the time through working long hours in other days of the week and half a day on every Saturday. In the remaining time of the weekend, I had to work towards my PhD. I was busy, working seven days a week, and there was no time to rest except sleeping a few hours at night.

With my wife and two children, I lived in a basement flat in East London for twenty-two months. No sunlight could be found within the flat. Whenever we were out, we could feel how beautiful the sun was. The daylights never felt so good – the absence of light in our basement flat helped me realise the value of sunlight as mercy of God.

Life was tough, but we enjoyed every moment. We experienced the beauty of love and trust amongst us. Both my wife and I got the opportunity to discover each other as a new person where I was no more a Lieutenant Commander with so many facilities, and she was not a naval woman. We had no time to think of the days we left behind. The adversities of life tested our character and helped us solidify our moral values. Faith, prayer, and patient perseverance survived our London dreams. My two sons learned the value of integrity, character and self-dignity. They learned how to chase dreams with faith in God; how to live with love, and never lose hope.

Hope keeps us dreaming. Love keeps us living. Faith keeps us moving – even when we cannot see the lights on the other side of the tunnel.

One day, I completed my PhD. My wife and two sons saw me receiving the certificate during the graduation ceremony at the University of Nottingham. I noticed hope in their eyes. A few years later, my older son graduated from LSE after completing his bachelor degree with a full scholarship. When I think of all these moments, I cannot control my tears. I can experience the blessings of God Who is "Most Gracious, Most Merciful" (Qur'an 1:1). His tests are opportunities for us to grow.

Questions:

1. Can you think of a situation in your life when you went through struggles?
2. What did you learn from this experience?
3. Did you take it as an opportunity to transform yourself and develop your moral character? What will you do in retrospect?

PART IV

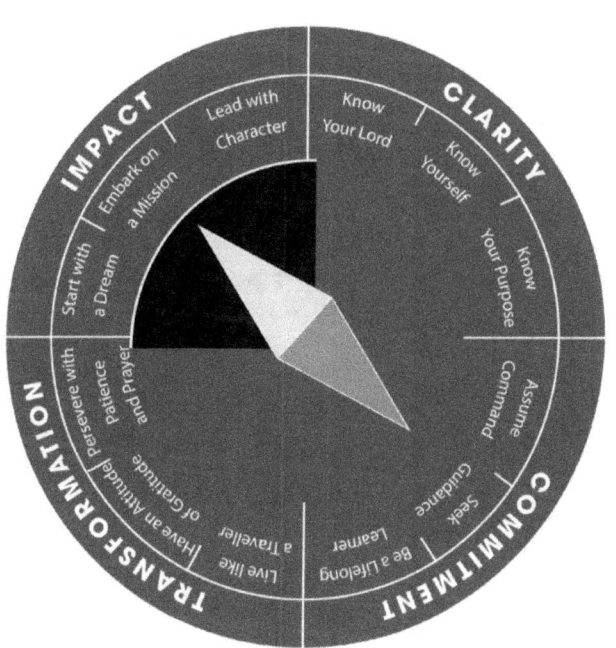

IMPACT

Far better it is to dare mighty things, to win glorious triumphs even though checkered by failure than to rank with those poor sprits who neither enjoy or suffer much because they live in the gray twilight that knows neither victory not defeat.

Theodore Roosevelt

10

START WITH A DREAM
Navigate with a Vision

A dream has always been very close to my heart. I can still remember my first day in college. Coming from a small town, I was very nervous when I was entering the classroom of one of the best colleges in the country. It was Dhaka College, named after the name of the capital city of Bangladesh. It was my dream that brought me to the capital city from a divisional town, and my father, despite his financial hardship, did not let my dream die. As I entered into the class, I was amazed to see Professor Abdullah Abu Sayeed, who was a well-known figure in the country due to his multiple identities as a writer, television presenter, organiser, and activist. He was also known for launching a "movement of reading" through creating mobile libraries on buses. However, I did not know that he was a professor at the college where I came to pursue my dreams. On my first day in the college, he inspired me with a fascinating quote of Luis Villalobos: *"You are only as big as your dreams."*

DREAM KNOWS NO LIMITS

Professor Abdullah Abu Sayeed taught me a great lesson: there should not be any limit on our dream. Compare the world today with the world a thousand years before – what does it tell us? The movers and the shakers of the world did not put any limit on their dreams. Thus, we are living in a world which is at its pinnacle of science, technology, creativity, innovation, art and commerce. It would never be possible had there been a limit on the dreams of people. We need to trust that if our dreams scare us, it is absolutely acceptable as Ellen Johnson Sirleaf says:

> "The size of your dreams must always exceed your current capacity to achieve them. If your dreams do not scare you, they are not big enough."

Ellen is right. Without scary dreams, it is challenging to take significant steps in life. Without taking steps outside of the comfort zone, our dreams never become realities. That is why the aerospace scientist who served as the 11th President of India defined 'dream' as something that does not let us sleep:

> "Dream is not that which you see while sleeping it is something that does not let you sleep" – A P J Abdul Kalam

A dream has the power to bring energy in life that keeps us going. Dreams extend our horizon and compel us to push the boundaries of possibilities. With loads of inspirations dreams help us to see all the shades of life. Dream gives us the audacity to look into the sky while we are standing on the ground!

Let Your Dreams Drive You

Since I left Professor Abdullah Abu Sayeed's class, I have been chasing my dreams – one after another. I was furthered moved by Martin Luther King, Jr.'s *"I Have a Dream"* speech. However, at some stage of my life when I felt spiritual emptiness, I turned to the words of God and read Surah Yusuf, the 12th Chapter of the Qur'an. This Surah introduced me with a real dream dreamt by a young boy of Egypt – Yusuf (PBUH) (named as Joseph in the Bible), one of the prophets of God.

> [Of these stories mention] when Joseph said to his father, "O my father, indeed I have seen [in a dream] eleven stars and the sun and the moon; I saw them prostrating to me. (Qur'an 12: 4)

This beautiful Surah ends with the interpretation of the dream, unfolding the history to us. He went through several struggles, but at the end, Yusuf (PBUH) became the finance minister, and later the king of Egypt. The teaching of Sūrah Yūsuf has profound leadership implications in our lives. The lesson that we can take away is: *our dreams can only come to reality through hardship and struggle*. The bigger the dream, the tougher the challenges. However, Joseph crossed all the difficulties one after another with uncompromising faith in God and through demonstrating one of the precious virtue of a leader: integrity of his moral character. Despite his exemplary character, he was humble and did not hesitate to acknowledge the weakness of his heart, seeking protection and guidance from his Lord.

> He said: "O my Lord! The prison is more to my liking than that to which they invite me: unless You turn away their snare from me, I should (in my youthful folly) feel inclined towards them and join the ranks of the ignorant." So his Lord listened to him (in his prayer), and turned away from him their snare: verily He hears and knows (all things)." (Qur'an 12:33 - 34)

Let Your Vision Drive Others

Everyone dreams. But leaders set themselves apart from the crowd by articulating their dreams into a compelling vision, envisioning others to see the future so clearly as if they are living in the future. One of the most significant attributes of leaders is the ability to articulate a vision that inspires actions. Leaders can see the potential in the future that others cannot. While leaders' dreams empower them to articulate a vision, their vision sets their people on a mission. Leaders know how to inspire, influence and mobilise. Great leaders have a great vision for their people. A great example is Prophet Ibrahim (PBUH), named as Abraham in the Bible, who had a great vision not only for him but for his land; and for his people - generation after generation. This was reflected through his supplication to his Lord, as mentioned in the Qur'an.

> And remember Abraham said: "My Lord, make this a city of peace, and feed its people with fruits,-such of them as believe in Allah and the last day." He said: "(Yea), and such as reject faith, - for a while will I grant them their pleasure, but will soon drive them to the torment of fire, - an evil destination (indeed)!" (Quran 2: 126)
>
> Our Lord! Send amongst them a messenger of their own, who shall rehearse Your signs to them and instruct them in scripture and wisdom, and sanctify them: For You are the Exalted in Might, the Wise. (Quran 2: 129)

The above verses explain that Ibrahim (PBUH) seek abundance for his people and at the heart of which was the guidance of his Lord to show light to his people. Allah was so pleased with his supplication that all the prophets came into his lineage, including the last Prophet, Muhammad (PBUH).

> And We gave (Abraham) Isaac and Jacob, and ordained among his progeny prophethood and revelation, and We granted him his reward in this life; and he was in the hereafter (of the company) of the righteous. (Quran 29: 27)

Vision has a profound leadership implication. Great leaders also use the vision to gain the commitment of their people for a significant cause. The question is how leaders communicate the vision to their people. In his book: "Lead with a Story: *A Guide to Crafting Business Narratives That Captivate, Convince and Inspire"*, Smith (2012) prescribed storytelling as a great way to communicate vision, and people with clarity of the vision are more inspired to be part of a movement than those who are not aware of it. But leaders need to master the art of storytelling to communicate their vision and get access to the hearts and minds of their people. In "The Secret Language of Leaders: How Leaders Inspire Actions Through Narrative", Denning gave a comprehensive analysis of how Al Gore was defeated in 2000 US presidential election for telling the wrong stories and not following the rules of storytelling. He then gave another account of Al Gore, where he learned the art of storytelling, which reflected through with his movie, "The Inconvenient Truth" and following speeches. Al Gore cracked the art of communication, and the secret was noting but telling the right story in the right way. Research shows how knowing the art of storytelling gives leaders an incredible advantage to connect with their people, and how storytelling creates meaning.

> "OUT FOR A WALK ONE MORNING, a woman came across a construction site where three men were working. Curious, she approached one of them and asked what he

was doing. Clearly annoyed she had bothered him, he barked, "Can't you see? I'm laying bricks!" Not easily put off, she asked the next man what he was doing. He responded matter-of-factly, "I am building a brick wall 30 feet tall, 100 feet wide, and 18 inches thick." Then turning his attention to the first man, he said: "Hay, you just passed the end of the wall. You need to take off that last brick." Still not satisfied, the woman asked the third man what he was doing. Despite the fact that he appeared to be doing exactly the same thing as the other two men, he looked up with excitement and said, "Oh, let me tell you! I am building the greatest cathedral the world ever known!" (Smith, 2012, p. 14)

What do you think about the level of motivation of these three men? Their motivation depends on the meaning their work makes in their life. Great leaders use stories to articulate the vision that people can relate to and create meaning that people quest for. Great leaders are not afraid to have their vision locked into heaven even they are standing on the ground. Indeed, if the leaders do not strive to take their people to heaven, their vision is shortsighted.

On your journey to purposeful leadership, you should have a clear vision not just for this world but for the eternal life as well. While you have several career goals, you need to make sure that the way you lead your life in this world paves the way towards heaven because that is the ultimate long-term success of life, which is sustainable as well.

> Every soul shall have a taste of death: And only on the Day of Judgment shall you be paid your full recompense. Only he who is saved far from the fire and admitted to the garden will have attained the object (of life): For the life of this world is but goods and chattels of deception."
> (Qur'an 3: 185)

CASE STUDY

Often a big dream or a passion sets us on a mission even if we do not have any resource to pursue them. This is the reasons many top companies in the world has started in the garage. But driven by their passion and dream, some people leave a lucrative career and comfortable life to take the challenge. Enamul Haque, a friend of mine, is an excellent example of this. Enamul is a seasoned IT professional with over twenty-six years of experience, working for many top companies in the world, including Nokia and Microsoft. He was part of many game-changing projects, and his clients include topnotch companies. He is fascinated with managing digital transformation and optimisation strategies, with sustained operational performance. His areas of expertise interest me as I teach creativity and innovation at the MBA level in a British University in London, and very interested to know what latest things are happening in the industries and how emerging technologies are changing the way we live and do business.

Enamul is an instant reference for all my doubts. He also

came to my university and delivered a specialised session for my students. Drawing on his experience of working for Nokia and Microsoft, and harnessing the power of storytelling, Enamul engaged the audiences with his wonderful and thought-provoking presentation. The students were immensely benefitted through his knowledge and experience – particularly the real-life examples he brought forward were of great sources of inspiration.

However, to pursue his dream of working for the top technology companies in the world, Enamul had to make a critical decision. After his Engineering degree in Computer Science from the University of Geneva, Enamul started a job with the United Nations High Commissioner for Refugees (UNHCR) and International Telecommunication Union (ITU) in Geneva. The salary was tax-free, and life was beautiful. He was quite steady in his career. In a word, everything was perfect, said Enamul.

Nevertheless, he could listen to a different song deep inside his heart. The possibility of emerging technologies to be a powerful driver to change the course of the world told him that he needs more challenges in life. He was not sure if he would be able to survive in the new job but he took a risk to join Nokia, which was one of the leaders in the technology industry at that time. Although Nokia is no more dominating the sector, Enamul has gone through different transformations in his career. Eventually, he worked for his dream companies and lead many technology projects, creating a huge impact.

> "I am totally fulfilled with what I have achieved in life, but it was possible by taking a step to come out of my comfort zone", Enamul said to me.

Recently, he authored a book, "Digital Transformation through Cloud Computing: Developing a sustainable business strategy to eschew extinction". He has also launched his YouTube channel to share his knowledge and experience with those who are passionate about digital transformation, data science and artificial intelligence.

Enamul's story teaches us the value of discovering our passion and how to chase our dreams. If you can align your job with your passion, soon you will find it has a meaning to yourself, and no wonder you will see your craft becoming an art. "If you love what you do and you are passionate about it, your mental health is sorted, which is the foundation of your wellbeing," Enamul said.

PLANNING THROUGH REFLECTIVE THINKING

1. Capture five dreams that are very close to your heart.

2. Find two compelling reasons for each dream. Why do they matter?

3. Turn your dreams into goals by adding a timeline to them. Remembers goals are SMART: Specific, Measureable, Achievable, Realistic and Time-bound. However, focus more on 'Time' and 'Monitor the Progress'.

4. Develop an action plan for each goal. Include daily, weekly and monthly activity and use Key Performance Indicators (KPI) to monitor your progress.

"It must borne in mind that the tragedy of life does not lie in not reaching your goals, the tragedy lies in not having any goals to reach. It isn't a calamity to die with dreams unfulfilled, but it is a calamity not to dream. It is not a disaster to be unable to capture your ideals, but it is a disaster to have no ideals to capture. It is not a disgrace not to reach the stars, but it is a disgrace to have no stars to reach."

Dr Benjamin Isaiah Mays

11

EMBARK ON A MISSION
Make Service Part of Every Day

While dreams and visions give us the clarity of where we are going, purpose and mission tell us why we are in this world, taking us on a journey towards our aspired destination. Vision inspires us with a dream-future; mission gives us the meaning and joy to take every step towards it. As God's lieutenant, we are not just here to exist. We are here to make a meaningful impact in the lives of other fellow human beings who are our brothers and sisters. We are here to make this world a better place for others who are living with us and who are yet to come when we are no longer in this world.

To support our living, we need to work, and all kinds of

jobs are respectable so long we make an honest earning. We need to make our craft meaningful too. The best way to do it is by serving humanity and other creations of God through the touch of our work. Not having absolute clarity about our mission, we often find our life worthless. We cannot see the value of our art – the work we do for a living. But the truth is we all born as heroes - as God's Lieutenants. It just needs a mission to set us on a hero's journey.

Clarity of mission helps us to see our art differently, giving us the pride and joy for what we do. A compelling mission helps us to find the meaning in our life not by our materialistic gains but by the impact we make in the world.

Vision sets us on a journey to success with our eyes towards heaven. Mission sets us on a journey to significance: to touch as many hearts and minds as we can through our work, creating our little paradise in this world. It helps us to live a life of fulfilment.

Psychologically, human beings are created in a way that they find true happiness at the service of others – often we do not ponder enough to understand that. Call it a mission or a reason, it is the urge to transform the way human beings live and work that sets Steve Jobs and Steve Wozniak on a mission to create the personal computer.

"Being the richest man in the cemetery doesn't matter to

me. Going to bed at night saying we've done something wonderful, that's what matters to me." Steve Jobs

Steve Jobs' confession clearly explains that he did not find the meaning of his life because of his wealth but because of the mission to serve humanity that started with the Apple's slogan:

"Think Different"

The size of his mission not only gave the courage to challenge IBM, the giant in the industry but also gave him the audacity to ask the then CEO of PepsiCo, John Sculley to join his team.

"Do you want to sell sugar water for the rest of your life, or do you want to come with me and change the world?" Steve Jobs

Can you imagine what gave this young entrepreneur the courage to talk with a CEO who was running a multibillion-dollar business? His vision sat him on a mission to change the way we live by harnessing the power of the personal computer. He eventually changed the way we live by bringing never-before-seen products, one of which is the smartphone that brought the world within our fingertips.

Sculley joined Apple when he could see a different world through the vision and mission of Steve Jobs that he had articulated for Apple. A noble mission attaches meaning to our work. The real value of our work is measured by the way we serve humanity. An exciting mission helps us find dignity in our work irrespective of our profession. Have you ever thought about how we can inspire a sweeper with a noble mission? Great leaders do it very well. Martin Luther King explains that a sweeper's job is an art and no less than a great painting, music, or poetry.

> "If a man is called to be a street sweeper, he should sweep streets even as a Michaelangelo painted, or Beethoven composed music or Shakespeare wrote poetry. He should sweep streets so well that all the hosts of heaven and earth will pause to say, 'Here lived a great street sweeper who did his job well." Martin Luther King Jr.

A great mission is one that helps people to seek excellence and see their work as a calling. We can find ourselves on the path to significance when our jobs become more significant than our job titles, allowing us to serve humanity. How would you define the roles that the nurses, doctors, frontline workers and backline workers are playing? It is time for us to value these people. If COVID-19 could not teach us that a nurse, a doctor, a bus driver, delivery man, a supermarket staff, a sweeper are not less important than a CEO, a world cup footballer, a movie star or an Olympic athlete, we need to question our conscience. In fact, they have played more prominent roles, letting the world function during this pandemic. To find meaning in our work, we need to develop an attitude of servitude: exploring all opportunities to serve humanity. Great missions differentiate true heroes who dedicate their lives at the service of others. We all know how John F. Kennedy created a sense of calling.

> "Ask not what your country can do for you – ask what you can do for your country".

This inspired many Americans to find a way to serve the nation – what a compelling mission! Great missions also differentiate the purpose-centric companies from the profit-centric ones. One example is 'Whole Foods' whose co-founder John Mackey – during an interview said: "We're not retailers with a mission, we're missionaries who retail" (Gallo, 2016, p. 53). When the 1981 Texas flood destroyed everything in the store, the management was ready to close the business. But they were amazed by the feeling of their employees and the customers.

> "The water destroyed everything in the store. The store's owners didn't have flood insurance and had no savings. Just when all seemed lost, something unexpected happened. The stores employees refused to let it die and its customers refused to let it go. They began to show up with mops, buckets, and shovels. The store's founders were amazed as dozens of people kept coming. "Why are you doing this" one of the founders asked a volunteer. "I am not sure if I would want to live in Austin if the store wasn't here. It's made a huge difference in my life," the customer said." (Gallo, 2016, p. 51)

This shows how great missions inspire businesses to makes a difference in the lives of their customers and employees. Similar was the case behind the success of

Starbucks when Howard Schultz re-defined its business.

> "We are not in the coffee business serving people, but in the people business serving coffee." Howard Schultz

Now, let us turn our question regarding the purpose of life from the perspective of Divine the message, i.e. the Qur'an. This will allow me to end this chapter talking about the greatest mission of all times, which was given by God to His Messengers starting with Adam (PBUH) to guide human beings so that they don't go astray. The last recipient of this mission was Prophet Muhammad (PBUH) who was the last and final messenger of God.

> "O you (Muhammad) wrapped up (in the mantle)! Arise and deliver your warning! And your Lord do you magnify!" (Qur'an 74:1-3)

This was the mission, setting Prophet Muhammed (PBUH) on a journey to invite people to submit to their Lord and to glorify Him. While the God-given purpose of life is to worship Him with the vision to be the inhabitants of heaven in eternal life, the mission is to manifest the purpose of life through the art of living. The success of a mission is not in its articulation instead in its manifestation. What could be a better mission than to submit to God and service to humanity, and helping others to do the same?

CASE STUDY

Often we do many good things for raising our image in the eyes of others and forget how we need to look after our parents when they need us. Let me tell you a story about one of my friends who was always with me as someone I can trust and share my thoughts and aspirations. His name is Hafiz Al Mujahid. I met Hafiz in Khulna in 1985, while studying in the last year of the high school. We had a lot of similarity in the way we think and live our shared values. While living in the hostel, we often talked until late nights, discussing how we could find some opportunities to study abroad. There was no internet at that time and accessing to information was not so easy. We were not very clear if we would be able to bring our dreams of studying abroad a reality. But we were determined to serve the country in some way. Joining the Navy turned out to be the best option for both of us. Navy allowed us to serve the nation. We were steering well in fair winds and following seas until we promoted to the ranks of Lieutenant Commander in the Navy. We never knew that fifteen years would pass so quickly. As I took voluntary retirement to try my luck on dry land, Hafiz followed me with an aspiration to migrate to Canada, something he was dreaming for a long time. While waiting for a decision for his Canadian migration application, he found a job of his passion within a non-profit organisation that was contributing to save lives in Bangladesh through their research on diarrhoea and other health-related diseases. His dedication and passion helped him jump onto his career ladder fast.

Then one beautiful afternoon, he received a letter from the Canadian High Commission.

> "With fear and anxiety, I opened it but could not control my tears", Hafiz said to me.

Finally, their dream to live and pursue a career in Canada came true. But, things happened very dramatically after that. When he discussed it with his wife, both of them realised that his parents were in their old age and Hafiz was the only son. He was confused, but a verse in the Qur'an helped him to make a significant decision of his life.

> "And your Lord has decreed that you worship none but Him. And that you be dutiful to your parents. If one of them or both of them attain old age in your life, say not to them a word of disrespect, nor shout at them but address them in terms of honour." (Qur'an 17:23)

They decided to let go of the opportunity, and Hafiz continued with his career in Bangladesh. Then what Hafiz told me was fascinating:

> "As I sacrificed my dreams for my parents, I started experiencing fulfilment in my life and success in my career that I never dreamed of."

A few months later, he called me to tell the decision of an application he made to Harvard. I could not believe what he said, but the news made my day. My friend is finally going to Harvard for a 6-month General Management programme with a full scholarship. Hafiz was sure that he was making a difference with his current job, but he firmly believes that all these were possible because his parents kept on raising their hands to God. During his time at Harvard, we talked almost every day - Hafiz was keen to share everything he was learning, and I was excited to know. Here is what Hafiz told to me:

> "HBS gave me a deep understanding of how business works and how to lead the organisational transformation, which remains as a valuable asset with me."

At Harvard, Hafiz met with Michael Porter and Bill George, both of whom are my favourite authors in strategy and leadership respectively and I could not wait to hear every detail of his learning experience. With new knowledge in his possession, Hafiz dared to make another career transformation and landed to United Nations World Food Programme (UNWFP). This makes his heart sing every night, as he knows he was supporting from behind the curtain a number UN Sustainable Development Goals. Recently, Hafiz has completed his 7- month long international assignment in Jordan. We also managed to meet in London and Rome to cherish the memories of our old days.

This story teaches a great deal of leadership. Leaders should have the courage and moral character to sacrifice and let go of their dreams for more significant causes. In the end, our Lord knows what is good for us, and He sets us on the road that allows us to transform the most.

REFLECTIVE QUESTIONS

1. What three small steps can you take to make a difference in this world, on a small scale?

2. Are you going to take these steps today?

   Remember, the beginning of a great journey start with a small step. Now is the best time to start.

3. Would you like to keep this initiative and attitude alive by taking three small steps every month?

   There are many people around us whom we can serve in many ways: through our knowledge, empathetic listening, time, money, love and compassion. Step on to the leadership ladder by making service part of everyday.

Most people find strength in things that are outside them: money, power, titles, wardrobes, cars. But most of the things that make a leader are on the inside: integrity, wisdom, confidence, vulnerability, joy, passion, compassion, intuition. These things come from life experience, from life's trials, from the deepest part of a person's soul. You can't fake them, and you can't buy what's not for sale.

John Hope Bryant
Love Leadership: The New Way to Lead in a
Fear-based World, p. 30

12

LEAD WITH CHARACTER
Bring Values to Life

A few years ago, I read a story about a bank robbery by only two robbers: one senior and the other was his accomplice. The senior robber never went to school, but the junior completed the A–level education. Initially, the employees in the bank wanted to resist them and safeguard the money of their clients under their disposal. However, the bank manager, who was a university graduate, asked the employees not to risk their lives by confronting the robbers. Instead, he let the robbers go away with the money they wanted. In a moment, he appeared to be a great leader to his people: someone who puts the lives of his people first. Hardly seen nowadays.

When these robbers came to a secure place, the younger member wanted to count the money they robbed. But the senior stopped him. Your school education did not teach you anything, the senior said. Wait, I will tell you the amount in a moment, he added. The younger robber was quite surprised and could not figure out how his boss would find the amount without counting. But when the TV news unveiled the amount to be $1 million, the senior proudly said the junior, "See, the experience is much more valuable than education." However, the junior, not being happy with the number, started counting the money. He counted them several times and found only one hundred thousand. The junior then told his boss: "You did not go to school and risked both of our lives only for one hundred thousand. But think about the bank manager who went to university and earned nine hundred thousand by fooling us." I believe you have already understood the moral of the story. A highly competent leader without character is a dangerous leader.

In this chapter, we will discuss the final pointer of the leadership compass. This is the most valuable leadership trait: character. We will also shed lights on the concept of *'leading with the character'* from an Islamic perspective drawing on the lessons from the Qur'an. This invaluable trait has been manifested through the lifestyle of the last prophet, Muhammed (PBUH).

CHARACTER: WHAT IT IS AND WHY IT MATTERS

The above story tells us a lot about the importance of character in all aspects of our lives. No matter how educated, knowledgeable, competent and visionary a leader is, if they lack character, they are not trusted.

> "The most valuable component of leadership is not power, position, influence, notoriety, fame, talent, gifting, dynamic oratory, persuasiveness, intellectual superiority, academic achievement, or management skill. It is *character*. Character is the cradle of credibility for the leader. Without the element of strong, noble, honorable character, leadership and all its potential achievements are in danger of cancellation. Every leader is as safe and secure as his character." (Munroe, 2014, p.5)

Character links to moral discourse, normative, and differentiates between right and wrong, should and ought, and good and evil (Bass and Steidlmeier, 1999). Character is the most precious wealth of a leader that earns them the trust of their followers.

According to Hannah and Avolio (2010), "a leader character is defined not only by what the leader thinks but also by his motivation to act" *(p. 929)*.

The character has a significant role to play both in *leadership* and *life. C*haracter enables us to do what is right under any circumstance, which echoes in the statement of the Greek philosopher, Socrates.

> "It is never right to do wrong or to requite wrong with

wrong, or when we suffer evil to defend ourselves by doing evil in return" Socrates

The character was always a subject of interest of the philosophers, including the great philosophers Aristotle and Plato. Character is the hallmark of good people, as Plato said:

> "Good people do not need laws to tell them to act responsibly, while bad people will find a way around the laws."

Character is not about talking good things but about doing those. According to Plato, the real character reveals when leaders act responsibly without being controlled by laws. Aristotle has supported Plato's view of character:

> "What the states is most anxious to produce is a certain moral character in his fellow citizens, namely a disposition to virtue and the performance of virtuous actions"

AN INTERDISCIPLINARY PERSPECTIVE OF CHARACTER

Nonetheless, as the focus of the organization is mostly on the bottom line of the income statement, the study of leader's character has mostly been overshadowed by the study of leader's competence (Sturm et al., 2017) with the perception that leader competence has a more significant influence on organizational performance. In the recent time, however, the research on leader's character has further gained attention during the financial crisis of 2008 – 2009 (Gandz et al., 2010), when the world has witnessed plays after plays performed by 'characters' one after another, who demonstrate everything but not the character. In his book, *'The Power of Character in Leadership: How Values, Morals, Ethics, and Principles Affect Leaders'*, Munroe (2014) gives a narration of this play:

> "In the dynamic drama of contemporary leadership playing on the world stage today, there are many "characters" who lack character. Moreover, the trail of history is littered with many would-be great men and women who harnessed the reins of power in various fields – political, social, economic, corporate, athletic, spiritual, and more. The wielded great influence and/ or control over the lives of others; many felt the weight of material wealth and fame – only to have it all disintegrate and blow away like dust in the wind because of their tragic deficiencies of character." (p.1)

Traditionally, moral character and moral behaviour are linked to ethical behaviour and ethical leadership (Sturm et al., 2017; Cohen et al., 2014) and conceptualised by six dimensions (Peterson and Seligman, 2004):

1. Wisdom
2. Courage
3. Humanity
4. Justice
5. Temperance
6. Transcendence.

Further studies by Crossan et al. (2015) and Seijts et al. (2015) have conceptualised character by eleven dimensions:

1. Judgment,
2. Transcendence
3. Drive
4. Collaboration
5. Humanity
6. Humility
7. Integrity
8. Temperance
9. Justice
10. Accountability
11. Courage.

These dimensions are rooted in several disciplines. However, there are still missing elements that can be drawn to conceptualise good character in light of the Divine scriptures. Recently, there has been quite a lot of academic research on '*spirituality in the workplace*' as business organisations facing overwhelming behavioural decay in the overall employee attitude, ranging from theft cases to sexual harassments (Kamil, 2011). Leaders failing to demonstrate ethical behaviour and moral character. As a result "The nations of the world do not lack people in leadership positions. They lack genuine leadership in their leaders." (Munroe, 2014, p.23).

Researchers interested in the character-driven, ethical leadership are consulting every possible source to conceptualise character, and the way leaders can develop it. However, it appears that they do not pay much attention to the Divine scriptures. God had been sending messages through His messengers to bring human beings from darkness to light. The Divine scriptures promote moral values, equality, and excellent behaviour through anchoring faith in God.

CONCEPT OF CHARACTER IN ISLAM

In the Qur'an, *righteousness* has often been used to signify good character, and Prophet Muhammed (PBUH) has been endorsed as the most exemplary character: *"And you (stand) on an exalted standard of character."* (Qur'an 68: 4). The Qur'an has provided a very comprehensive definition of righteousness.

> It is not righteousness that you turn your faces towards east or west; but it is righteousness to believe in Allah and the last day, and the angels, and the book, and the messengers; to spend of your substance, out of love for Him, for your kin, for orphans, for the needy, for the wayfarer, for those who ask, and for the ransom of slaves; to be steadfast in prayer, and practice regular charity; to fulfil the contracts which you have made; and to be firm and patient, in pain (or suffering) and adversity, and throughout all periods of panic. Such are the people of truth, the Allah-fearing. (Qur'an 2:177)

If we carefully read this verse, we can notice that formation of righteousness starts with the belief – particularly belief in God and the last day (Day of Judgment) – and ends with God–fearing. The righteous leaders believe that their Lord monitors their actions. They will be accountable on the Day of Judgment, if not in this world, for their deeds. While emphasising the leadership implication of righteousness as mentioned in the above verse, Beekun and Badawi, (1999, p. 21) have deduced several moral attributed of Muslim leaders:

1. They act justly and do not allow their personal feelings to hamper justice.
2. They take care of those in need and do so for the love of Allah.
3. They are steadfast in prayer and practice charity.
4. They observe all contracts and do not break their word.
5. They are patient and firm, no matter what adversity or personal suffering they may be experiencing.

To be more precise, the Arabic word for the character is Akhlaq, which is composed of three dimensions according to some Islamic scholars.

1. Ethics
2. Good conduct
3. Morality.

Akhlaq also refers to the practice of virtue, morality and good manners. Character, which encompasses morality, is possibly the most essential virtue of a leader. Following Hadith establishes a link between faith and morality.

> On the authority of Abu Hurayrah (RA), who said: The Messenger of Allah SWT said, "The most complete of the believers in faith are those with the best character [and

morals]." Abū Dāwud, Tirmidhī and Darimī (Mishkāt, Book of Etiquette, Hadīth no. 5101; Book of Marriage, Hadīth no. 3264) (Hasan, 2009, p.83)

Drawing on several Hadiths, Hasan (2009) has identified some aspects of good personal character (p. 98–113), which include the following:

1. Self–Control
2. Forgiveness and Forbearance
3. Magnanimity
4. Hayā (Modesty, Shame, Shyness)
5. Dignity and Solemnity
6. Keeping Secrets
7. Humility
8. Humility and Self-Effacement
9. Avoiding Fame
10. Contentment
11. Simplicity in Lifestyle
12. Moderation
13. Constancy
14. Generosity
15. Honesty and Trustworthiness

While explaining leadership from an Islamic perspective, Beekun and Badawi (1999) have developed a model that incorporates four layers of moral character in Islam. These show various stages where the leaders and followers can be in their journey.

1. Iman
2. Islam
3. Taqwa
4. Ihsan

Iman

Iman refers to affirmation in the six articles of faith that include faith in:

1. Allah
2. His angels
3. His books, i.e. Divine scriptures: Qur'an is the last and final message from God
4. His messengers
5. Day of Judgement
6. Divine Decree about good and evil

Beekun and Badawi (1999) go on saying that at the core of Islamic moral character is Iman and at the heart of Iman is the belief in the *Oneness of Allah* (Tawhid) and the prophethood of Muhammad (PBUH). *Iman*, with its all six articles of faith, enables leaders to realise that the ultimate success is in the eternal life and the results of our deeds in this world will be unveiled on the Day of Judgement by Allah. Thus, leaders with Iman, lead with a very long *long–term–mindset*, which is beyond our death.

Islam

Islam refers to acquiring peace through willful submission to our God, Allah (Beekun and Badawi, 1999). Islam is the practical manifestation of Iman through five pillars:

1. Shahada (The Testimony of Faith)
2. Salah (Obligatory Prayers)

3. Zakat (Obligatory Charities)
4. Siyam (Obligatory Fasting)
5. Hajj (Pilgrimage)

Taqwa

Taqwa is the consciousness of Allah, which has at least two dimensions:

1. The fear of Allah
2. The awe of Allah

This is a precious characteristic of a believing leader who not only submit to his Lord through Islam but also develop awe of Allah:

> "all-encompassing, inner consciousness of one's duty toward Him and the awareness of one's accountability toward him" (Beekun and Badawi, 1999, p. 19)

Taqwa facilitates the people and leaders proactively manifest complete Islam while enjoying the test of Iman and avoid the injunctions given by Allah.

Ihsan

Ihsan refers to the love of Allah. This is a state of a believer when "the love of Allah" motivates the individuals to work toward attaining Allah's pleasure. The following Hadith describes Islam, Iman and Ihsan well.

On the authority of 'Umar b. al-Khattab, (RA), who said: Whilst we were sitting with the Messenger of Allah,

(PBUH) that day, a man appeared before us. His clothes were extremely white, his hair intensely black. No trace of travelling was visible upon him, and none of us knew him. (He proceeded) until he sat before the Prophet, (PBUH), placing his knees and his palms upon his thighs. He then said, "O Muhammad! Tell me about Islam [Submission]." He replied, "Islam is that there is no god except Allah, and you establish the Salat [Prayer] and pay the zakat [Alms-tax], fast Ramadan and make the pilgrimage to the House if you able to find a way to do that." He said, "You have spoken the truth." We were amazed at him: asking him and then confirming what he said. He said, "Then tell me about Iman [Faith]." He replied: "[Iman is] that you have faith in Allah, His angels, His Books, His Messengers and in the Last Day, and you have faith in Predestination: its Good and its Evil." He said, "You have spoken the truth." He further said, "Then tell me about Ihsan [Excellence]." He replied, [Ihsan is] that you worship Allah as though you could see Him. But if you are not able to see H, then He sees you" He said, "Then tell me about the Hour." He replied, "[Its sign are that slave-woman gives birth to her mistress, and you see barefoot, naked, destitute shepherds competing in the constructions of lofty buildings." He then departed. I stayed for a long while, after which he said to me, "O 'Umar, do you know who the questioner was?" I "Allah and His Messenger know best." He said, "It was Jibril [Gabriel]: he came to teach you your religion." Muslim (Mishkat, Book of Faith,

Hadith no. 2) (Hasan, 2009, p.31-32)

Now, one may ask, what is the implication of Iman, Islam, Taqwa, Ihsan on leadership in general and leading with character in particular? The answer is not so complicated. The different levels of consciousness of leaders involving mind and body (through the practice of Iman and Islam) and mind and heart (through the manifestation of Taqwa and Ihsan) make the leaders accountable to God.

As leadership is about influencing the behaviour of followers through power and authority (McCall, 1978), many leaders, as we can see, have manipulated their people for their personal gains. Week leaders have used power because of a sense of insecurity and lack of belief upon themselves. On the other hand, leaders who manifest genuine Iman through Islam, Taqwa and Ihsan do not manipulate their followers due to the fear and consciousness of Allah and their accountability on the Day of Judgement.

> On that day will men proceed in companies sorted out, to be shown the deeds that they (had done). Then shall anyone who has done an atom's weight of good, see it! And anyone who has done an atom's weight of evil, shall see it. (Qur'an 99: 6-8)

Leaders' bases of power is divided into two categories (Beekun and Badawi, 1999):

1. Position power, which includes legitimate, coercive and

information power; and
2. Personal power, which includes expert, referent and prestige or reputational power

Again, leaders who manifest genuine Iman through Islam, Taqwa and Ihsan know that the sovereignty only belongs to God: Allah is the Lord, and they are the slaves of their Lord and servant of their people. This was demonstrated by the fourth caliph of Islam, Ali ibn Abu Talib (RA) while he sent a letter to the new governor of Egypt:

> "Malik, you must never forget that if you are a ruler over them, then Caliph is a ruler over you, and Allah is the supreme Lord over the Caliph." (Beekun and Badawi, 1999, p.21)

The power of Iman, Islam, Taqwa and Ihsan give righteous leaders moral courage to protect their character by not compromising with anyone or anything in the world. They get moral courage due to consciousness of their Lord, which says to do what is right in all situation. While leading with character, the role models are the messengers of God.

Every messenger of God had the most exemplary character of their time, and there was one thing that they all shared. They submitted to their Creator and preached the truth concerning the One and Only God, showing people the right path to God and the strategy to achieve the ultimate success in the eternal life.

However, the last messenger of God who brought the final Divine message for the humankind is Prophet Muhammad (PBUH). We need to turn to him to learn what ideal character a leader should demonstrate. In the Qur'an, Allah has honoured His last messenger in several ways.

Allah introduced him as *"The Perfect Exemplar"* for humankind: "You have indeed in the Messenger of Allah a beautiful pattern (of conduct) for any one whose hope is in Allah and the final day, and who engages much in the praise of Allah." (Qur'an 33:21)

Allah symbolised him as *"The Embodiment of Mercy"* for all His creations: *"We sent you not, but as a mercy for all creatures."* (Qur'an 21:107)

Allah called him as *"The Radiant Light"*: *"O Prophet! Truly We have sent you as a witness, a bearer of glad tidings, and a warner - And as one who invites to Allah's (grace) by His permission, and as a lamp spreading light."* (Qur'an 33: 45-46)

Thus, there are great leadership lessons in the life of Prophet Muhammad (PBUH), which can inspire us to lead by character. In this regards, we can adopt a number of way to learn from his character.

1. We can love him and his principles (Reverence)
2. We can live by his teachings (Adherence)
3. We can follow his footsteps (Emulation)

4. We can take him as a role model and strive to acquire the qualities (Prophetic Substance) he has demonstrated.

He should be our inspiration in developing our character. A few of the most admirable qualities of Prophet Muhammad (PBUH) were his honesty, integrity and truthfulness. This is why even his enemies who wanted to kill him many times, used to keep their valuables to him for safeguarding. They knew that Muhammad (PBUH) would protect their valuables even by his life. In his book, '*The Leadership of Muhammad*', John Adair[4], has dedicated a chapter on Muhammad's (PBUH) 'trustworthiness':

> "During his hidden years in Mecca working with merchant-caravans, probably as a caravan leader, Muhammad acquired a new name: al-Amin, the Trustworthy One. The same root incidentally, gives the English word amen, often used at the end of prayers, an expression of hearty approval. We can only guess what it was about the character or conduct of Muhammad that gave rise to this attractive sobriquet, but there is a clue. In 622, while making ready for his migration from Mecca, Muhammad – in danger of his life – delayed long enough to dispose of some moneys that had been deposited at his house." (Adair, 2010, p. 59)

There are many stories captured by both Muslims and

---

[4] John Adair is the first leadership professor of the world who has trained more than a million managers on leadership and leadership development.

non-Muslims from the life of Prophet Muhammad (PBUH), showing that many people were attracted by the beauty of his character and embraced Islam.

LEADERSHIP IMPLICATION: AN ISLAMIC PERSPECTIVE

In Islam, a leader is seen as the *"Servant of God and His creations"* (Kriger and Seng, 2005, p. 774). While traditional leadership research focuses on traits, skills, behaviour, power, influence, organisational effectiveness (Yukl, 1989), the Islamic perspective of leadership starts with *leaders' accountability (1) to God* and (2) the people they serve. Thus, leaders in Islam are not concerned about their position or authority. Instead, they are more interested in the *rights of the people they are entrusted to serve.*

Leadership in Islam is also viewed as a trust (Beekun and Badawi,1999) placed upon the leaders by their people. Islam promotes two types of leadership: (1) Servant-leadership and (2) Guardian-leadership, meaning leaders are both servants and guardians of their followers (Beekun and Badawi, 1999).

Beekun and Badawi (1999) assert that as a servant, leaders should pursue the welfare of their people and guide them towards good (genuine success). On the other hand, as guardian, leaders need to protect their community from any kinds of tyranny and oppression.

They should also promote justice and encourage God-consciousness (*Taqwa*) in their people so that they can achieve the ultimate success in eternal life.

EPILOGUE

AHOY!

Congratulations! You have just completed reading all the twelve transformational steps that can set you on a journey to becoming a purposeful leader. It shows that you have a burning desire in your heart to become a leader driven by purpose.

- *When you stand in front of the mirror, do you see a leader?*
- *Do you meet God's Lieutenant on earth?*

There is no doubt that you are a leader as God's Lieutenant on earth. Before you know yourself, you need to know your Lord for He is your Creator. So, put God first in everything you do. Once you know your Creator discover why He has created you. That's your purpose – the moral gyro of your life. Your 'moral gyro' will guide you when you take passages through the grey areas of life.

> "If you are guided by an internal compass that represent your character and the values that guide your decisions, you are going to be fine. Let your values guide your actions and don't ever lose your internal compass, because everything isn't black or white. There are a lot of gray areas in business." (George and Sims, 2007, p. xxiv)

There are thousands of things happening to us that we cannot control, but we can choose our attitude. We can decide the way we will respond. Our leadership begins by assuming the command and taking the helm of our lives. To be able to steer the right course of our lives, we need to consistently seek the guidance of our Lord, and embark on lifelong learning to develop our third eye: *The Gut* that enables leaders to see beyond the horizon.

Remember, if we cannot find abundance in less, we need to rethink our values. True happiness comes through giving and not by increasing our possessions. What's the point of piling up things and make our simple life complex when we know that in this world we all are mere travellers: we have to leave when our time is up. Unless we develop an attitude of gratitude, we will not experience the uncountable blessings of God upon us. After recovering from COVID-19, when an old patient in Italy, saw the bill for using the ventilator, he started crying. When doctors inquired, he said that he was crying not for the bill, but for the oxygen, that God has given him free throughout his life. So, we should focus our eyes on the prize of life that keeps us alive.

The success of a leader is not determined by the number of their followers: even Hitler had many followers, but his genocidal campaigns meant he failed the test of 'character' and the purpose of life. Dare to have a big dream that will scare others but start small and start now. All the strategies and planning matter only if we take action. "There is a moment in every person's life when the awareness of their destiny bursts like a bubble onto the surface of their conscious mind. It is then that the weak avoid the realisation and busy themselves with the mundane tasks of their lives. It is also at that moment that the strong will awake and decide to take action to change their world for better and thereby secure themselves their rightful and valued place in the history of humankind." (Thompson, 1998, p.3). Life is short and time is precious. Make every moment count. Every moment is either a missed opportunity or a seized one that can make us either a failure or success. The world is waiting for you to lead. Prepare yourself and embark on a mission: make service part of every day. Every day is a new beginning – to develop yourself as a purposeful leader and make an impact in the lives of others. Remember, 'character' is the most precious treasure of men and women, and – of course – of leaders. Our character is developed by going through the tests (struggles) of life. When faced with struggles, we put our character to test and solidify our moral values. The challenges of life let us go through a purification process. 'Character' is the real charisma. Through character leaders win the most valuable prize: the trust of their people.

Ahoy! It's time to take action. It's time to submit to our God and serve His creations, including our fellow human beings. The miracle happens when we take action. Failure is not a defeat, it is an experience that prepares us to succeed.

REFERENCES

THE JOURNEY

Adair, J. (2010). *The Leadership of Muhammad*, London: Kogan Page

Asrar-ul-Haq, M. and Anwar, S. (2018). The many faces of leadership: Proposing research agenda through a review of literature, *Future Business Journal*, 4 (2), pp. 179-188

Bennis, W. G., an Nanus, B. (1985). *Leaders: Strategies for taking charge*. New York: Harper & Row.

Conger, J. A. and Kanungo, R. N. (1987). Toward a behavioral theory of charismatic leadership in organizational settings, *Academy of Management Review*, 12 (4), pp. 637-647

Fieldler, F. E. (1967). *A theory of leadership effectiveness*, New York: McGraw-Hill

Hart, M. H. (1989). *The 100: A Ranking of the Most Influential Persons in History*, New York: Citadel Press

House, R. J. (1976). *A 1976 Theory of Charismatic Leadership*, Toronto: University of Toronto, Faculty of Management Studies

Humphreys, J. H. (2001). Transformational and transactional leader behaviour, *Journal of Management Research*, 1 (3), p. 149

Northouse, P. G. (2009). *Introduction to Leadership: Concepts and Practice*, Los Angeles: Sage Publications

Northouse, P. G. (2007). *Leadership: Theory and Practice*, Thousand Oaks: SAGE Publications

Qur'an 21: 107 | 67: 2 | 66: 6 | 4:59 | 2:2

Sahīh Muslim 746 available on
https://abuaminaelias.com/dailyhadithonline/2012/08/11/prophet-character-quran/ (accessed on 06 June 2020)

Thompson, P. (1998). *The Pinnacle Principle: How to Maximise Your Potential*, London: Simon and Schuster Ltd.

Wren, J. T. (1995). *The leader's companion: Insights on leadership through the ages*, New York: Free Press

Yukl, G.A. (2010). *Leadership in Organizations*, Upper Saddle River: Prentice Hall

THE LEADERSHIP COMPASS

Dobbs, R., Manyika, J. and Woetzel, J. (2016). *No Ordinary Disruption: The Four Global Forces Breaking All the Trends*, New York: PublicAffairs

Munroe, M. (2014). *The Power of Character in Leadership: How Values, Morals, Ethics, and Principles Affect Leaders*, New Kensington: Whitaker House

Qur'an 2: 30-32 | 21:16 | 39: 9 | 68:4 | 96: 1-4

Moin, S. M. A. (2019). *The Purpose of Life: Understanding the Divine Message through the Lens of Leadership and Strategy*, Amazon.com, Inc.: Kindle Direct Publishing

Welch, J. and Welch, S. (2005). *Winning*, London: HarperCollins*Publishers*

KNOW YOUR LORD

Jammer, M. (1999). *Einstein and Religion: Physics and Theology*, New

Jersey: Princeton University Press

Qur'an 1:5 | 2:22, 127-129, 138, 255 | 3:8, 3:190 |6:101 |7:180 |20:8 | 21:33 |32: 9 |57:3 | 59: 22-24 |67: 3-4 | 75: 22-23 | 112: 1-4

Zakariya, A. (2015). The Eternal Challenge: A Journey Through The Miraculous Qur'an, London: one reason

KNOW YOURSELF

Al-Ghazali, S. M. (2005) A Thematic Commentary on the Qur'an, London: The International Institute of Islamic Thought (Translated by Ashur A. Shamis and Revised by Zaynab Alawiye)

Jawaid, M. (2010). Evolution of the Soul, *academia.edu*, available on Google Scholar

Jawaid, M. (2019). The Faculties for Guidance, *academia.edu*, available on Google Scholar

George, B. and Sims, P (2007). True North, Discover Your Authentic Leadership, San Francisco: John Wiley & Sons, Inc.

Moin, S. M. A. (2019). *The Purpose of Life: Understanding the Divine Message through the Lens of Leadership and Strategy*, Amazon.com, Inc.: Kindle Direct Publishing

Qur'an 2:30 -39, 155 -157 | 7:20, 179 | 12:53 | 16: 2, 102 | 17:85 | 18: 1-3 | 22: 46 | 26: 83-89 | 32:9 | 39:53 |89:27-30 |91: 8-10

KNOW YOUR PURPOSE

George, B. and Sims, P (2007). *True North, Discover Your Authentic Leadership*, San Francisco: John Wiley & Sons, Inc.

Qur'an 3:185 |6: 76-79 | 8: 2 - 4 |19: 42-50 | 23: 1- 11, 115 |

49:13 | 51: 56 |52: 35 |67: 1-2 | 78: 8-11 | 103: 1-3

ASSUME COMMAND

Clark, R. T. (2016). Leading with Character and Competence, Oakland: Berrett-Koehler Publishers, Inc.

Northouse, P. G. (2013) Leadership: Theory and Practice (Sixth Edition), London: Sage.

Clark, T.R. (2016). Leading with Character and Competence, Oakland: Berrett-Koehler Publishers, Inc.

Smith, P. (2012). Lead with a Story: A Guide to Crafting Business Narratives That Captivate, Convince and Inspire, New York: American Management Association

Tracey, B. (2014). Leadership New York: American Management Association

SEEK GUIDANCE

Khan, N. A. (2013). Light upon Light, Bayyinah Institute, available on https://www.youtube.com/watch?v=6dMllapsjP8, accessed on 08 June 2020

Qur'an 1: 1-7 | 2: 1-5, 155-157, 255, 257 | 3: 102 | 5: 15-16 | 8: 29 | 17:15 | 14:1-4 | 24: 35 | 99: 6-8 | 112:1-4

BE A LIFELONG LEARNER

Bucaille, M. (2003). *The Bible, the Qur'an and Science: The Holy Scriptures Examined in the Light of Modern Knowledge.*

Jami` at-Tirmidhi, Vol. 5, Book of Knowledge, Hadith 2687 available on *https://muflihun.com/tirmidhi/41/2687* (accessed on 07 June 2020)

Qadhi, Y. (2015). The Humility of Knowledge Vs. The Arrogance of Ignorance, available on
https://www.youtube.com/watch?v=6JgLxVPStJ8 (accessed on 08 June 2020)

Qur'an 1:6-7 | 2: 31-33, 21:107, 164, 255 | 3:18, 185 | 6: 106 | 17:14 | 20: 114 | 35:28 |39:9 | 49: 13 |59:18 | 67: 2 |102:1-8

Sahih Al-Bukhari: Vol 1, Book 3, Hadith 79 available on https://sunnah.com/bukhari/3 (accessed on 07 June 2020)

Seijts, G. (2013). *Good leaders learn: Lessons from lifetimes of leadership*. London: Taylor and Francis Ltd.

Sunan Abi Dawood, Vol. 4, Book of The Office of the Judge, Hadith 3634 available on *https://muflihun.com/abudawood/25/3634* (accessed on 07 June 2020).

Sahih Muslim 746 available on
https://abuaminaelias.com/dailyhadithonline/2012/08/11/prophet-character-quran/ (accessed on 07 June 2020)

Sunan Abu Dawood Book 18 Hadith 2879 *available on* https://sunnah.com/abudawud/19/1 (accessed on 07 June 2020)

LIVE LIKE A TRAVELLER

Draper, B. (2012). *Less is More*, Oxford: Lion Hudson plc.

Qur'an 3:14 | 62:10 |66:6 |67: 3-4 | 69: 25-37 | 102:1- 8

Steve Jobs' Stay Hungry, Stay Foolish Speech at Stanford (2005), available on *https://singjupost.com/full-transcript-steve-jobs-stay-hungry-stay-foolish-speech-at-stanford-2005/* (last accessed on 02 July 2019)

HAVE AN ATTITUDE OF GRATITUDE

Qur'an 1:1-7 | 14: 7 | 16:18 | 23:78 | 31: 12 | 35: 12 | 78: 6-16

PERSEVERE WITH PATIENCE AND PRAYER

Qur'an 2:30, 2:36, 153, 286 | 21: 83-84, 87-88| 29:2 |*31:17-19* | 37: 139-148 | 67: 2 | 93:1-11

Menk, M. (2011). Sabr (The Virtue of Patience) available on https://www.youtube.com/watch?v=ADiTs-ZXuhw (accessed on 07 June 2020)

Sahih Muslim 2999, available on https://abuaminaelias.com/everything-decreed-is-good-for-the-believer-both-ease-and-hardship/ (accessed on 07 June 2020)

Sunan al-Tirmidhī 2499 available on *https://abuaminaelias.com/dailyhadithonline/2014/01/20/best-sinners-repentance/* (accessed on 07 June 2020)

START WITH A DREAM

Quran 2: 126, 129 | *Qur'an 12: 4, 33 – 34* | Quran 29: 27

Smith, P. (2012). *Lead with a Story: A Guide to Crafting Business Narratives That Captivate, Convince and Inspire*. New York: American Management Association

EMBARK ON A MISSION

Gallo, C. (2016). *The Storyteller's Secret: How TED Speakers and Inspirational Leaders Turn Their Passion into Performance*, London: Macmillan.

Qur'an 74:1-3

LEAD WITH CHARACTER

Adair, J. (2010). *The Leadership of Muhammad*, London: Kogan Page

Bass, B. M. and Steidlmeier, P. (1999) Ethics, Character, and Authentic Transformational Leadership Behavior, Leadership Quarterly, 10(2), 181-217.

Beekun, R. I. and Badawi, J. (1999). *Leadership: An Islamic Perspective*, Beltsville: Amana Publications

Bryant, J. H. (2009). Love Leadership: The New Way to Lead in a Fear-Based World, San Francisco: Jossey-Bass

Cohen, T. R., Panter, A. T., Turan, N., Morse, L. A., & Kim, Y. (2014). Moral character in the workplace. *Journal of Personality and Social Psychology*, 107 (5): 943-963

Crossan, M., Seijts, G., and Gandz, J. (2015). *Developing leadership character*. New York: Routledge.

Gandz, J., Crossan, M., Seijts, G. and Stephenson, C. (2010) Leadership on Trail: A manifesto for leadership development. London, ON: The Richard Ivey School of Business.

Hannah, S. T., & Avolio, B. J. (2010). Moral potency: Building the capacity for character-based leadership. *Consulting Psychology Journal: Practice and Research*, 62(4), 291-310.

Kamil, N. M., Al-Kahtani, A. H., and Sulaiman, M. (). The Components of Spirituality in the Business Organizational Context: The Case of Malaysia, *Asian Journal of Business and Management Sciences*, 1 (2): 166-180

Kriger, M. and Seng, Y. (2005) Leadership with inner meaning: A contingency theory of leadership based on the worldviews of five religions, *The Leadership Quarterly*, 16 (5), pp. 771-806

Munroe, M. (2014). *The Power of Character in Leadership: How Values, Morals, Ethics, and Principles Affect Leaders*, New Kensington: Whitaker House

Peterson, C., & Seligman, M. E. P. (2004). *Character strengths and virtues: A classification and handbook.* New York: Oxford University Press.

Qur'an 2:177 | 21:107 | 33:21, 45-46 | 68: 4 | 99: 6-8

Seijts, G.,Gandz,J.,Crossan,M., and Reno,M. (2015). Character matters: Character dimensions' impact on leader performance and outcomes. *Organizational Dynamics*, 44, 65–74.

Sturm, R. E., Vera, D. and Crossan, M. (2017). The entanglement of leader character and leader competence and its impact on performance, *The Leadership Quarterly*, 28 (3): 349 – 366

Yukl. G (1999) An evaluation of conceptual weaknesses in transformational and charismatic leadership theories, *The Leadership Quarterly*, 10, pp. 285-305

Hasan, A. A. G. (2009). The Way of the Prophet: A Selection of Hadith, Licestershire: British Islamic Foundation

EPILOGUE

George, B. and Sims, P (2007). *True North, Discover Your Authentic Leadership*, San Francisco: John Wiley & Sons, Inc.

Thompson, P. (1998). *The Pinnacle Principle: How to Maximise Your Potential*, London: Simon and Schuster Ltd.

INDEX

Abraham 63, 88, 142, 203
Adam 69, 70, 71, 74, 145, 146, 181, 190, 216
Admiral ix, 25, 26, 27, 28, 109, 110, 111, 113
Affective 74
Africa 36
Air Force 44
Alexander 166
Al-Fatihah 119, 120
Allah 14, 15, 39, 43, 45, 47, 50, 53, 54, 55, 57, 58, 59, 60, 61, 62, 63, 64, 69, 71, 72, 75, 76, 77, 79, 80, 83, 88, 89, 90, 91, 92, 94, 96, 97, 98, 116, 117, 118, 119, 121, 123, 124, 125, 126, 128, 129, 132, 133, 134, 135, 136, 137, 138, 139, 143, 145, 146, 147, 149, 150, 156, 160, 162, 163, 165, 167, 173, 175, 177, 178, 181, 182, 183, 184, 185, 186, 187, 189, 190, 191, 192, 193, 194, 203, 229, 230, 231, 232, 233, 234, 235, 236, 237
Almsgiving 91
Arabia 141
Aristotle 226
Army 44, 101

Bangladesh ix, 23, 25, 82, 93, 101, 109, 126, 152, 171, 199, 217, 218, 255
Beauty 11, 44, 47, 55, 60, 151, 155, 156, 160, 170, 171, 195, 239
Behavior 12
Bengali 3, 22
Bible 89, 148, 201, 203, 248
British 206, 252

Cadet 101, 131, 170
Captain 27, 83, 93, 101, 102, 114, 168, 169, 170
CEO 31, 46, 140, 213, 214
Character viii, 15, 16, 20, 24, 30, 45, 46, 47, 48, 86, 111, 112, 114, 138, 148, 183, 184, 188, 192, 193, 194, 195, 196, 202, 220, 224, 225, 226, 227, 228, 229, 230, 231, 232, 235, 236, 237, 238, 239, 242, 243, 246, 249, 251, 252, 253
Charisma viii, 24, 47, 193, 244
Charity 21, 35, 96, 121, 229, 230
Civilisation 142, 148
Clarity 4, 10, 16, 17, 39, 40, 42, 51, 64, 68, 86, 97, 162, 204, 211, 212
Clarity v, 40, 49
Coach 9, 24, 103, 155
Cognitive 74
Commander 25, 27, 28, 168, 195, 217, 255
Commitment vii, 16, 28, 37, 38, 42, 78, 94, 139, 204
Commodore 25, 27, 28, 29, 93, 152, 168
Conative 74
Courage viii, 4, 23, 26, 43, 158, 213, 220, 236
COVID 174, 214, 243
Creator vii, viii, 12, 39, 41, 42, 45, 51, 52, 54, 55, 57, 58, 59, 60, 61, 64, 65, 67, 72, 83, 87, 89, 90, 91, 97, 117, 119, 121, 125, 128, 134, 135, 136, 138, 141, 143, 145, 146, 147, 148, 149, 163, 164, 173, 175, 176, 192, 236, 242, 253

Death vi, 3, 7, 8, 9, 10, 12, 13, 17, 36, 70, 83, 94, 95, 98, 122, 125, 126, 137, 160, 161, 165, 166,

253

182, 206, 232
Defence 27, 83
Dhaka 23, 199
Divine vi, vii, 5, 6, 7, 13, 15, 16, 38, 39, 51, 64, 68, 72, 73, 76, 82, 83, 87, 89, 92, 120, 126, 136, 138, 141, 142, 145, 147, 148, 149, 154, 155, 156, 163, 216, 228, 229, 232, 237, 246, 247

Earth 13, 38, 39, 40, 41, 44, 52, 53, 56, 58, 59, 60, 61, 64, 66, 67, 68, 69, 70, 72, 82, 89, 90, 92, 116, 117, 118, 123, 124, 125, 126, 129, 134, 141, 146, 147, 149, 162, 167, 174, 181, 182, 184, 191, 214, 242
Education 27, 33, 38, 133, 139, 223, 224, 253
Equality 229, 253
Eternal vi, 7, 8, 9, 10, 12, 13, 14, 90, 95, 96, 97, 122, 125, 126, 127, 133, 139, 162, 163, 167, 184, 205, 216, 232, 237, 240
Eternal 50, 53, 57, 64, 147, 165, 247
Ethics 227, 230, 246, 251

Facebook 19
Faith v, 3, 30, 43, 61, 117, 128, 129, 195, 233, 234
Fasting 91, 233
Forgiveness 79, 88, 97, 122, 137, 184, 189, 190, 193
Freedom v, 43, 117, 120
Frigate 25, 101, 131, 168, 169

Gabriel 141, 143, 235
Geneva 207
God iii, v, vii, 3, 5, 6, 10, 12, 13, 14, 15, 16, 17, 20, 21, 23, 29, 38, 39, 41, 42, 43, 44, 47, 51, 53, 54, 55, 57, 58, 59, 60, 62, 63, 64, 65, 67, 68, 69, 70, 71, 72, 73, 74, 78, 80, 82, 83, 88, 89, 91, 92, 93, 94, 96, 103, 118, 119, 121, 122, 126, 127, 128, 129, 135, 137, 138, 141, 142, 143, 145, 147, 150, 154, 160, 162, 163, 171, 174, 176, 177, 181, 182, 183, 186, 187, 188, 190, 193, 195, 196, 201, 202, 211, 212, 216, 219, 229, 230, 232, 235, 236, 239, 240, 242, 243, 244
Grateful 93
Gratitude 45, 174, 175, 177, 178, 188, 193, 243, 253
Guidance 117, 119, 248

Hadith 15, 136, 138, 145, 148, 150, 151, 156, 190, 193, 194, 230, 234, 235, 248, 249, 252
Harvard 219
Humanity vii, 21, 36, 41, 42, 46, 96, 146, 212, 213, 214, 216
Humankind vii, 5, 13, 16, 58, 68, 70, 73, 74, 78, 88, 92, 118, 123, 128, 135, 137, 138, 141, 142, 146, 151, 154, 165, 167, 171, 173, 174, 181, 182, 183, 185, 189, 237, 244

Iblis 69, 70, 71, 78
Ibrahim 74, 83, 88, 89, 125, 203
Iman 80, 178, 232, 233, 234, 235, 236
Insurance 31, 194, 215
Integrity 20, 24, 111, 113, 183, 195, 202, 222, 238, 253
Internet 19
Isaac 88, 203
Islam 27, 134, 135, 136, 138, 141, 150, 168, 178, 193, 231, 232, 233, 234, 235, 236, 239

Jacob 88, 203
Jesus 142
Jordan 219
Judgment 10, 12, 17, 74, 90, 94, 95,

119, 128, 137, 162, 177, 183, 206, 228, 230

Kennedy 215
Knowledge vii, 16, 24, 26, 27, 30, 33, 34, 35, 38, 43, 48, 58, 59, 65, 69, 75, 76, 88, 95, 104, 106, 110, 127, 132, 133, 134, 135, 136, 137, 138, 139, 141, 143, 144, 145, 146, 147, 148, 149, 150, 154, 155, 156, 164, 171, 207, 208, 219, 221

Leadership vi, vii, viii, ix, 4, 5, 6, 7, 9, 10, 11, 12, 13, 14, 16, 17, 18, 20, 22, 23, 24, 25, 27, 30, 31, 32, 34, 35, 36, 38, 39, 40, 42, 44, 45, 48, 51, 67, 72, 81, 82, 83, 85, 87, 102, 106, 107, 108, 109, 110, 111, 112, 113, 114, 126, 151, 154, 159, 169, 171, 186, 188, 189, 202, 204, 205, 219, 220, 221, 224, 225, 227, 228, 230, 231, 235, 237, 238, 239, 243, 245, 246, 249, 251, 252, 255
Lieutenant v, vii, 24, 29, 41, 67, 68, 72, 73, 82, 83, 195, 217, 242, 255
Life vi, vii, viii, ix, 3, 4, 5, 6, 7, 8, 9, 10, 12, 13, 14, 15, 16, 17, 18, 22, 23, 24, 25, 30, 31, 37, 38, 41, 42, 43, 44, 45, 46, 48, 51, 52, 60, 68, 69, 70, 71, 72, 73, 76, 81, 82, 83, 85, 86, 87, 89, 90, 91, 92, 94, 95, 96, 97, 98, 101, 103, 104, 113, 114, 117, 118, 120, 121, 122, 124, 125, 126, 127, 128, 129, 133, 134, 137, 138, 139, 140, 142, 144, 145, 147, 148, 149, 151, 152, 154, 156, 159, 160, 161, 162, 163, 165, 166, 167, 168, 170, 171, 174, 175, 176, 178, 181, 182, 183, 184, 185, 187, 190, 191, 192, 193, 194, 195, 196, 200, 201, 203, 205, 206, 207, 208, 210, 212, 213, 215, 216, 218, 222, 225, 232, 237, 238, 239, 240, 242, 243, 253
Lifeboat 30, 43
London 8, 27, 104, 105, 194, 195, 206, 219, 245, 246, 247, 248, 249, 250, 251, 252, 253, 255
Lord v, vii, 4, 10, 13, 39, 41, 42, 44, 47, 52, 53, 60, 62, 63, 64, 65, 66, 68, 70, 71, 72, 73, 74, 76, 77, 78, 79, 80, 88, 89, 91, 93, 95, 96, 97, 119, 120, 121, 122, 123, 125, 128, 130, 134, 135, 138, 141, 142, 144, 150, 162, 163, 165, 167, 172, 174, 175, 177, 178, 181, 184, 187, 188, 189, 190, 191, 202, 203, 216, 218, 220, 230, 233, 236, 242, 243, 253

Management viii, 4, 8, 9, 30, 31, 32, 34, 42, 151, 154, 215, 225, 255
Marine 44
Martin Luther King 86, 201, 214
Mecca 238
Mercy 5, 29, 59, 63, 71, 77, 79, 88, 93, 122, 128, 134, 142, 143, 150, 173, 174, 176, 177, 178, 184, 189, 192, 195, 237, 253
Microsoft 140, 206, 207
Midshipman 4, 25, 27, 101, 168
Military 30, 82, 109, 166, 186, 255
Monotheism 63, 64
Moral v, 42, 85, 251
Moses 142
Motivation 11, 35, 205, 225
Muhammad 5, 6, 14, 22, 44, 47, 68, 72, 91, 92, 118, 121, 135, 141, 142, 144, 145, 171, 203, 216, 232, 234, 237, 238, 239, 245, 251
Muslim 15, 63, 135, 139, 148, 194, 230, 235, 246, 249, 250

Nafs 75, 77, 78, 79, 80
Navigate v, 46, 199
Navy ix, 4, 23, 25, 26, 28, 29, 30, 33, 37, 81, 93, 101, 102, 104, 107, 108, 109, 110, 111, 112, 113, 126, 152, 169, 170, 217, 255

Nottingham 106, 195, 255

Olympic 4, 214

Pain 184, 229
Patience v, 45, 180, 188, 250
Perseverance 23, 185, 186, 188, 191, 193, 195
Pilgrimage 91, 233
Plato 105, 106, 226
Power vi, 10, 11, 17, 19, 20, 43, 47, 55, 59, 64, 69, 74, 95, 96, 97, 102, 105, 106, 120, 125, 126, 128, 133, 135, 148, 149, 154, 164, 167, 178, 189, 201, 207, 213, 222, 225, 227, 235, 236, 239
Prayers 91, 233
Prophet 5, 14, 15, 44, 47, 63, 72, 74, 83, 88, 89, 91, 92, 118, 121, 135, 138, 139, 141, 142, 144, 145, 146, 149, 151, 186, 187, 188, 189, 190, 191, 192, 203, 216, 229, 234, 237, 238, 239, 252
Psychology 94, 103, 177
Punishment..72, 122, 172, 177, 181, 192
Purpose vi, vii, 8, 10, 12, 17, 18, 20, 38, 41, 42, 46, 51, 68, 71, 72, 83, 86, 87, 89, 90, 91, 92, 94, 97, 105, 117, 124, 136, 145, 147, 148, 160, 162, 163, 165, 175, 182, 194, 211, 215, 216, 242, 243

Qur'an 5, 6, 13, 14, 15, 29, 38, 39, 43, 45, 47, 50, 52, 53, 54, 55, 56, 57, 58, 59, 60, 62, 63, 66, 68, 69, 70, 71, 72, 74, 75, 76, 77, 78, 79, 80, 83, 84, 88, 89, 90, 91, 92, 94, 95, 96, 97, 98, 116, 117, 118, 119, 120, 121, 122, 123, 125, 127, 129, 130, 132, 133, 134, 135, 136, 137, 138, 139, 141, 142, 144, 145, 147, 148, 149, 150, 154, 160, 162, 163, 164, 165, 166, 167, 172, 173, 174, 175, 177, 181, 182, 183, 184, 185, 186, 187, 188, 189, 190, 191, 194, 196, 201, 202, 203, 206, 216, 218, 224, 229, 232, 235, 237, 246, 247, 248, 249, 250, 252

Reality 8, 10, 46, 102, 103, 110, 124, 132, 133, 160, 163, 164, 165, 202, 217
Reason 145
Relationship 11, 12, 13, 32, 35, 37, 41, 65, 87, 102, 110, 119, 128, 147, 153, 168
Repentance 71
Research 34, 37, 52, 55, 74, 75, 77, 83, 92, 105, 106, 107, 108, 121, 127, 156, 177, 217, 226, 228, 239, 245
Researcher 107, 255
Responsibility vii, 4, 28, 33, 42, 43, 72, 82, 104, 107, 114, 117, 152, 182
Result 103
Robin Hood 106

Satan 69, 70, 78, 88, 181
Schultz 216
Science viii, 12, 20, 22, 75, 140, 148, 200, 208
Scripture 7, 13, 38, 39, 52, 68, 72, 83, 87, 145, 148, 154, 203
Secular vii, 6, 16, 44, 145, 146, 147,

154
Sermon 145
Silicon Valley 127, 154
Slave vii, 13, 62, 65, 119, 128, 189, 234
Socrates 11, 104, 105, 106, 107, 108, 109, 147, 168, 225, 226
Soul 42, 73, 74, 75, 77, 78, 79, 80, 83, 94, 95, 137, 144, 150, 175, 184, 206, 222
South Africa 36
Stanford 161, 249
Starbucks 216
Steve Jobs 22, 30, 37, 160, 161, 212, 213, 249
Strategic 69
Strategy 4, 7, 9, 16, 30, 31, 32, 126, 127, 133, 138, 139, 151, 154, 208, 219, 236, 255
Submission 120, 234
Substance 24, 229

Texas 215
Torah 89

Transformation v, 44
Traveller v, 44
Traveller 159, 249

Universe vii, 51, 53, 54, 55, 57, 58, 59, 64, 83, 87, 90, 93, 95, 102, 120, 121, 123, 128, 141, 253
University 32, 34, 44, 104, 105, 106, 139, 207, 223, 224
USA 127
Useful 94

Vision 8, 9, 20, 46, 55, 132, 133, 151, 160, 164, 179, 202, 204, 205, 213, 216

Wisdom viii, 7, 38, 44, 63, 69, 74, 80, 81, 89, 113, 133, 146, 148, 149, 154, 156, 175, 191, 203, 222, 253
Worship 62, 73, 79, 88, 91, 92, 119, 131, 142, 175, 177, 182, 192, 216, 218, 234

ACKNOWLEDGMENT

First of all, my sincere gratitude and thanks to my Creator and the Lord of the universe. Without His unconditional and uncountable mercy and blessings, I would not be able to complete this book.

My heartiest thanks to my wife and two sons for their, heart-melting love, generous support and exceptional patience while I was busy writing this book and could not look after them properly. You all are the inspiration for what I am doing and the challenges I am taking. I am also indebted to my father and my teachers, who have taught me the universal values of equality, compassion, integrity, honesty, self-respect. My father also explained the importance of character as the most essential attribute of a human being, and reminded me of the well-known quote by Billy Graham: "When wealth is lost, nothing is lost; when health is lost, something is lost; when character is lost, all is lost." His teachings and demonstration of a simple lifestyle with very little demand from life, has shaped my values, helping me find abundance in less. I am also indebted to my elder brother, M A Zaman, without whose unconditional love, support and guidance, I could never pursue my dream and be the person I am today. He is the true hero of my life. My gratitude to my other sisters and brothers, and to my mother – without whose support I could not complete my school education.

My special thanks and sincere gratitude to Jonathan Groucutt for sharing his pearls of wisdom about teaching and learning. Jonathon was my former Head of Department at Coventry University London, who helped in finding my academic identity. Jonathan was extremely kind to spare his precious time to read every chapter of this book and provided me with his valuable feedback. His feedback helped me reflect on various points more critically, which has clearly made a positive difference in the outcome of the book.

THE AUTHOR

Moin is an interdisciplinary researcher and a published author in brand storytelling, creativity, innovation, leadership and strategy. He spent fifteen years in the Bangladesh Navy, willingly retiring as a Lieutenant Commander. His military career was followed by ten years in several UK industries, including media, publishing, and financial services. As a management consultant, Moin has advised various companies and worked for the world's largest newspaper. In addition, he has worked as part of a $4 billion international subsea project. He has also served as an LEA Governor of the London Borough of Hounslow.

Moin then made a third transformation to academia. Currently, he is an Associate Professor in Marketing at the Queen Mary University of London. Before this, he worked as the Associate Head of Research and

Scholarship, University Ethics Lead and Vice-Chair of the Research, Scholarship and Ethics Panel at Coventry University London. He is a Fellow of the UK Higher Education Academy and Chartered Management Institute. He is also a reviewer of several academic journals.

He earned an MBA from the University of Strathclyde and a PhD in Management from the University of Nottingham. In addition, he has completed several courses in leadership, management, creativity and entrepreneurship from the Universities of Oxford, Cambridge and Harvard. While in the Navy, he trained at the US Defense Institute of International Legal Studies, the US Navy Atlantic Command, and the US Coast Guard's Leadership & Quality Institute and Command & Operations School.

Photo Credit: Orhan Demirovski

www.ingramcontent.com/pod-product-compliance
Lightning Source LLC
Chambersburg PA
CBHW060825220526
45466CB00003B/980